I0805063

Blue Ribbon Techniques

POWERTOOLS

CARE AND USE

William Veasey

Schiffer Publishing Ltd

1469 Morstein Road, West Chester, Pennsylvania 19380

Photography by noted wildlife photographer Tricia Veasey.

Library of Congress Catalog Number: 85-61523.

Printed in the United States of America.

ISBN: 0-88740-047-7

Published by Schiffer Publishing Ltd.

1469 Morstein Road, West Chester, Pennsylvania 19380

Designed by Ellen J. Taylor

This book may be purchased from the publisher. Please include $1.50 postage. Try your bookstore first.

Dedication

To all who have reversed a screw or shortened a shaft when it needed lenghtened.

Acknowledgments

The hands of the following:

Paul Suarez
Michael Veasey
Shirley Sizemore
Jeff Ebel
Michele Mosco

Purpose: To acquaint beginning carvers with a working knowledge and care of the basic power carving tools.

Foreword

One of the best power tools for carvers is a flexible shaft machine, consisting of an electric motor which drives a handpiece by means of a protected flexible shaft. A control provides continously variable speed. Hundreds of accessory points, burs, brushes, buffs, cutters and abrasives are available for use in material removal and finishing operations on almost any material. There are many handpieces, each of which can easily be connected to the flexible shaft, together with the wide variety of accessories, allows you to grind, carve, drill, sand, debur, engrave, polish, rout and brush with ease, speed and precision.

Some basic do's and don'ts

1. Do select quality equipment
2. Don't over lubricate
3. Do clean frequently
4. Do select equipment that "fits" your hand
5. Do always wear eye protection
6. Do not use worn out bits
7. Do not *force* equipment
8. Do allow the tools to work for and with you
9. Do develop rhythms and routines in tool use
10. Do use tools in manner for which they were designed
11. Do keep bits securely tightened
12. Don't be uncomfortable in *usage*

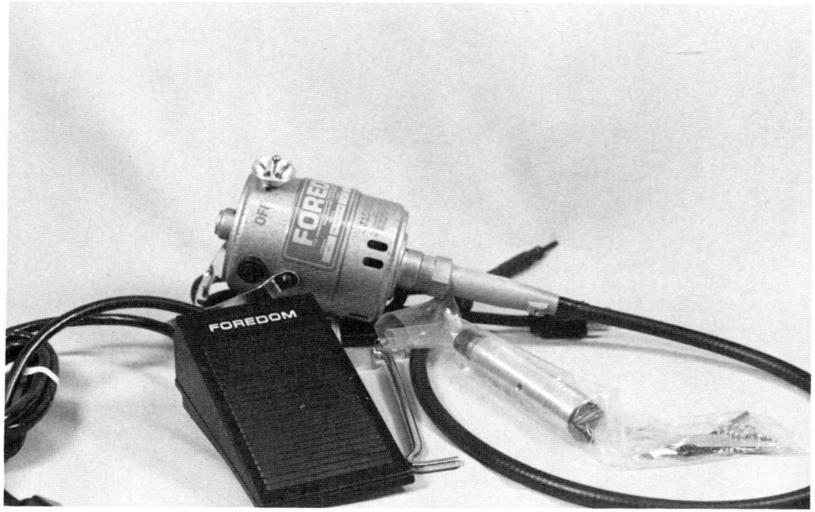

Foredom model CC with SCE foot control and 44B (1/4 capable) handpiece

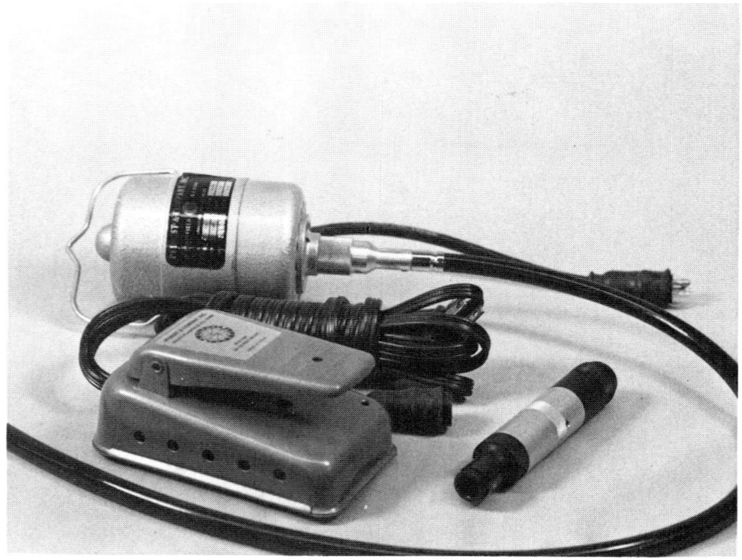

Pfingst flexable shaft machine with foot control and 1/4 (collet) handpiece

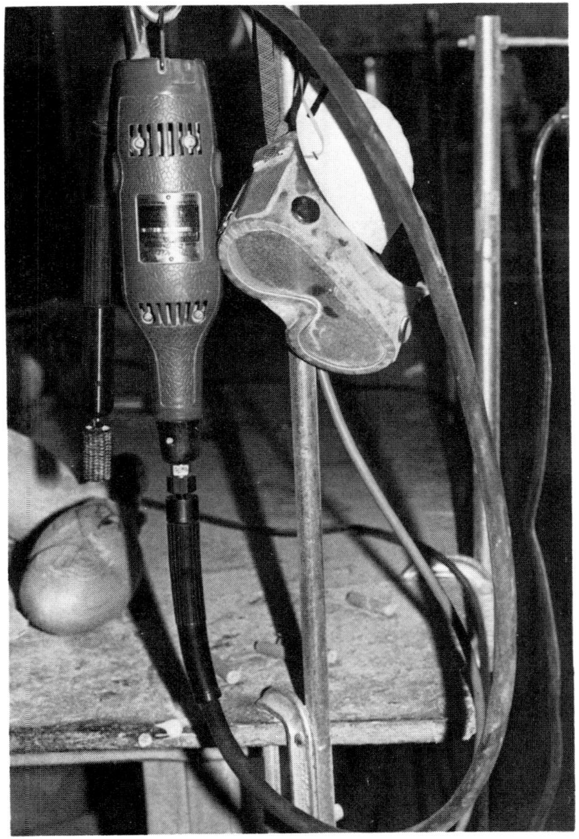

Makita die grinder with flexable shaft (also useful without shaft-direct drive) 1/4 handpiece built into heavy shaft for high speed and heavy grinding

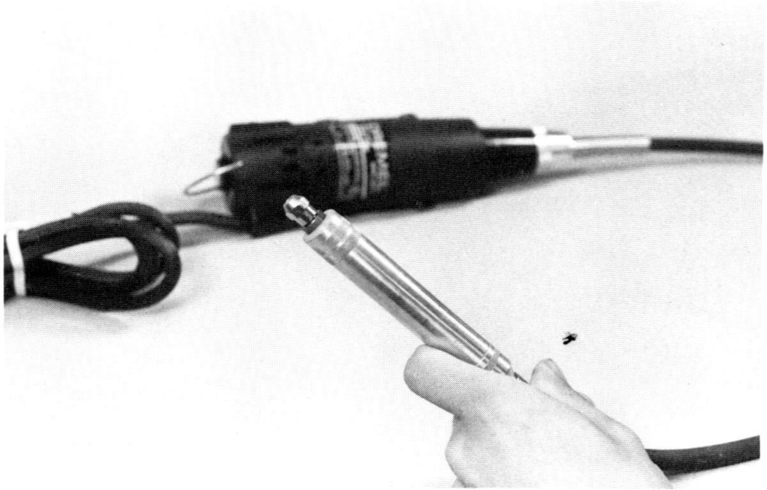

Dremel tool with flexable shaft and 1/8 and smaller collet—great for high speed texturing or shaping with ruby or diamond cutters (carvers) also works better with foot control

Same tool with assortment of small grinders and sanders—dental bits are particularly useful with Dremel. Many dentists will give you old bits which are no longer good for them but are still great for using with wood.

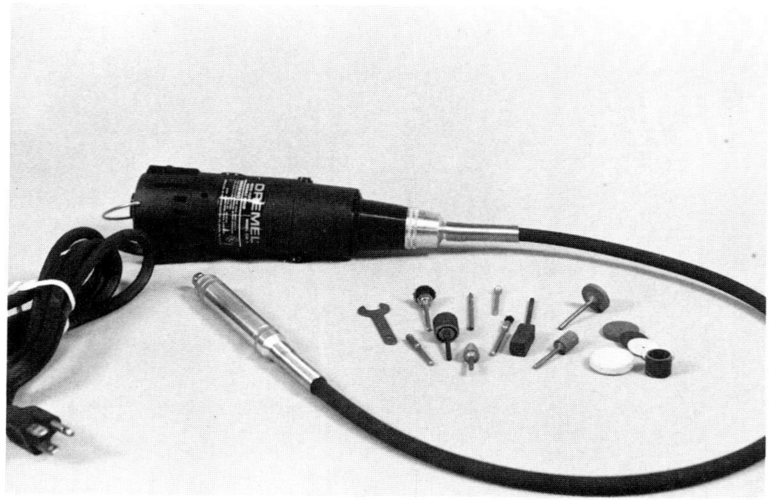

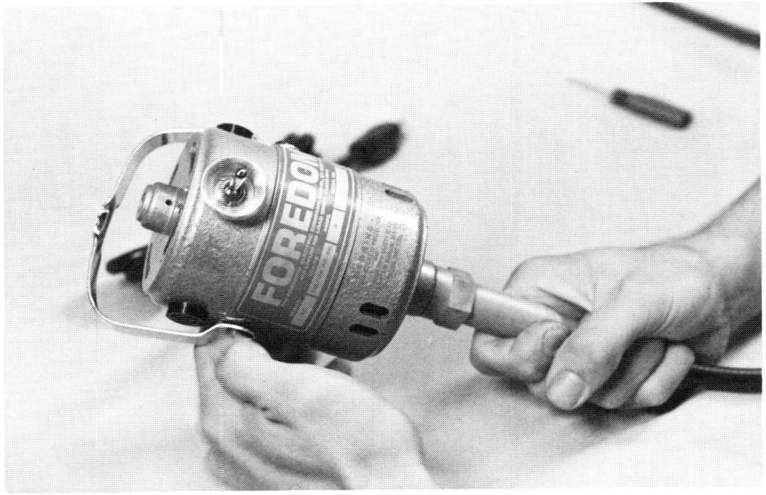

Collar which holds sheath to motor is left-handed or backwards threaded.

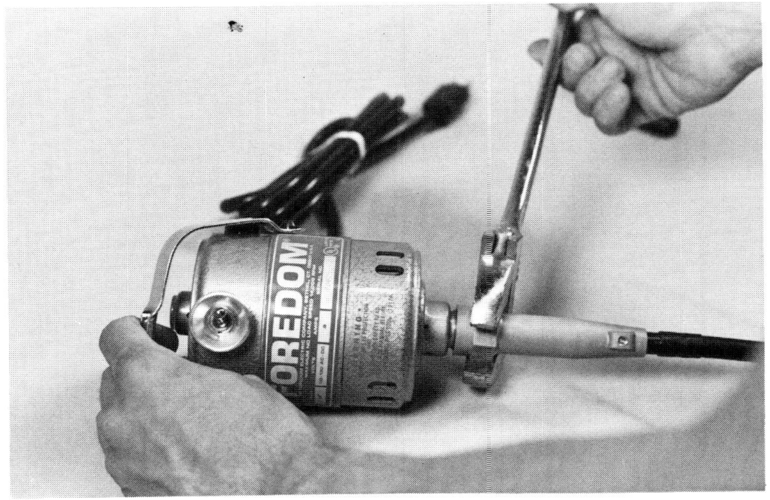

If collar is too tight to hand loosen use small adjustable wrench. Do not overtighten as most of these collars are plastic and can be broken, however, they are replacable.

Example—removing sheath from shaft
Example—shaft removed

Example—loosen screw on shaft to remove from motor
Example—replacing sheath

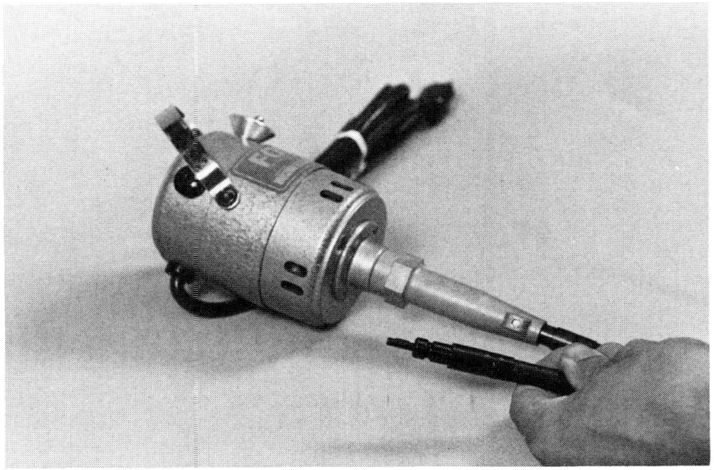

Example—important that approximately 1" of shaft extend beyond sheath. Example—is short

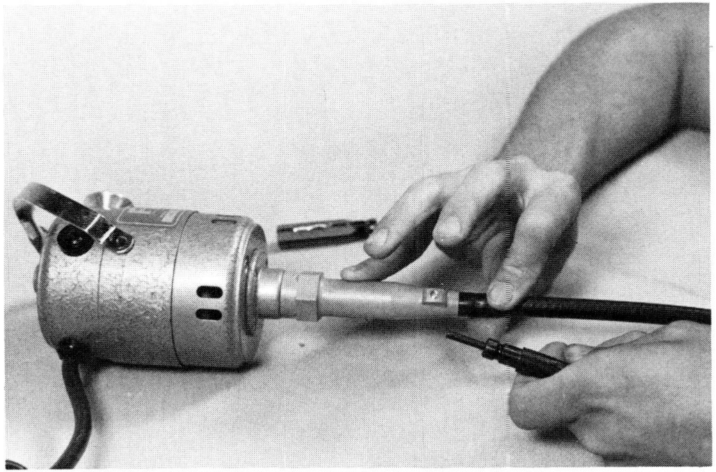

Example—adjustment screw on collar to extend or shorten sheath to accommodate this 1" on shaft

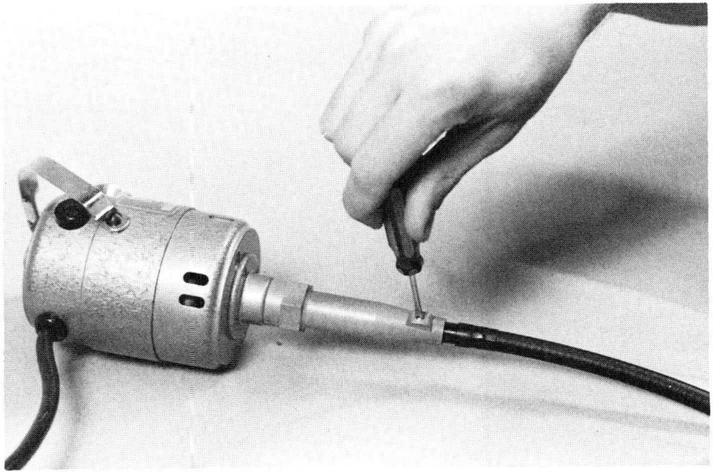

Example—corrected length of exposed shaft

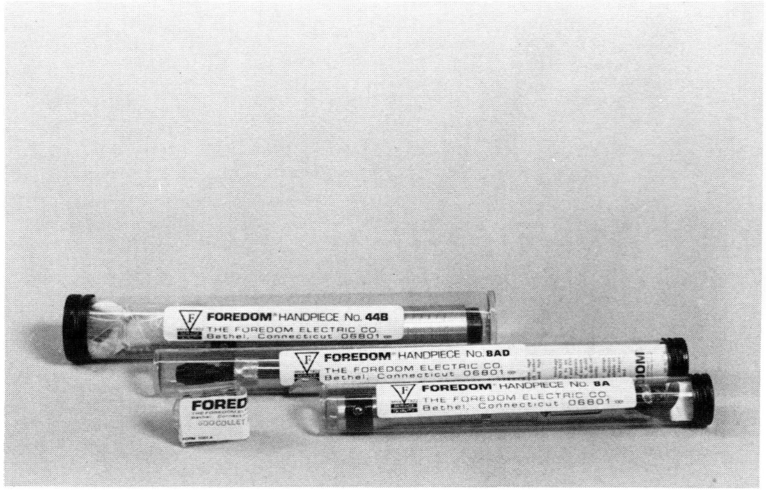

Example—assortment of foredom handpieces (also fit Pfingst and Cyclone machines)

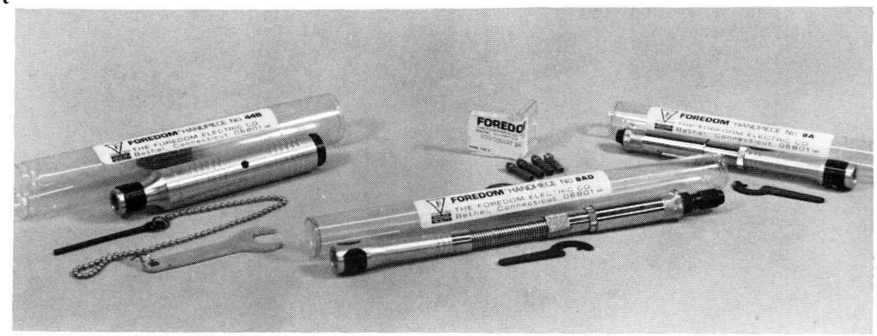

Example—assortment of handpieces 44B - 30 - 8 - 8D most used.

NO POSTAGE
NECESSARY
IF MAILED
IN THE
UNITED STATES

BUSINESS REPLY CARD

FIRST CLASS Permit No. 24 EXTON, P.A.

Postage will be paid by

SCHIFFER PUBLISHING, LTD.

BOX E

EXTON, PENNSYLVANIA 193419990

WE HOPE THAT YOU ENJOY THIS BOOK.....and that it will occupy a proud place in your library. We would like to keep you informed about other publications from Schiffer. Simply fill in and mail this postage-free card today.

TITLE OF BOOK: ______________________ ☐ hardcover
☐ paperback

☐ Bought at: ______________________
☐ Received as gift

COMMENTS: ______________________

____

☐ *Please add my name to your mailing list to receive information about books on:*

1. ☐ Porcelain
2. ☐ Photography
3. ☐ Gardening
4. ☐ Metal
5. ☐ Self help
6. ☐ Dolls
7. ☐ Toys
8. ☐ Architecture
9. ☐ Nature
10. ☐ Cooking
11. ☐ Decoys
12. ☐ Glass
13. ☐ Antique furniture
14. ☐ Wood carving

☐ *Please send me a FREE copy of the latest catalog of Schiffer Books.*

Name ______________________

Address ______________________

City ______________ State ________ Zip ________

SCHIFFER BOOKS ARE CURRENTLY AVAILABLE FROM YOUR BOOKSELLER

Printed in U.S.A.

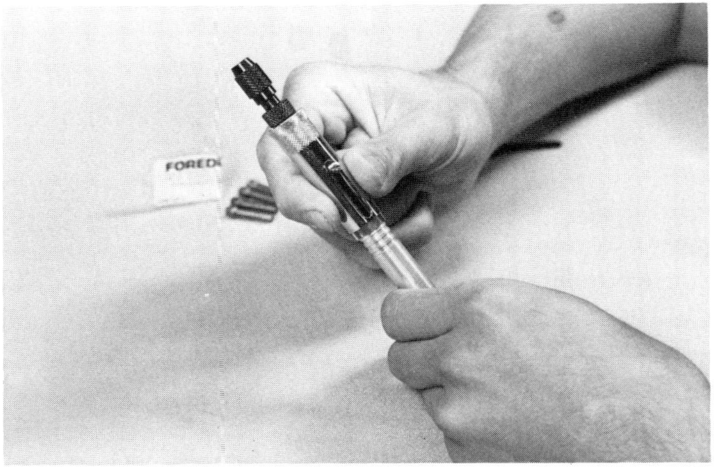

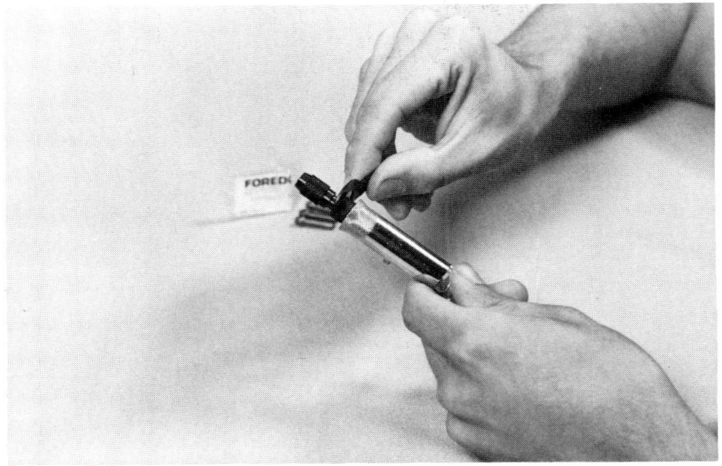

Example—series of steps in changing collets to accommodate different shank sizes of various bits for use in the 8 or 8D handpiece—which is the most common and easiest handpiece for use in detailing

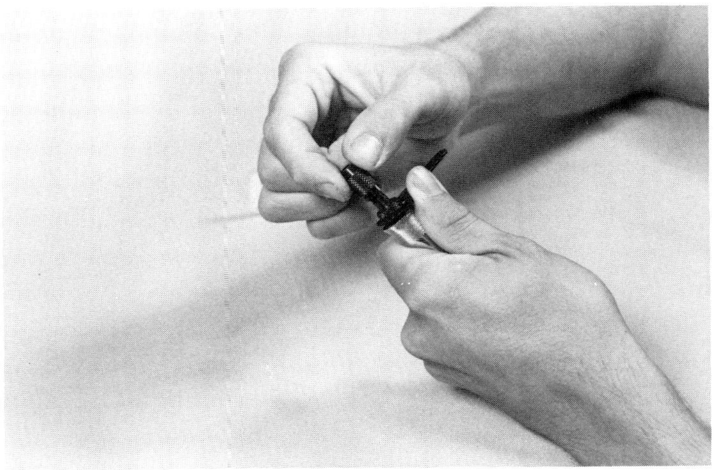

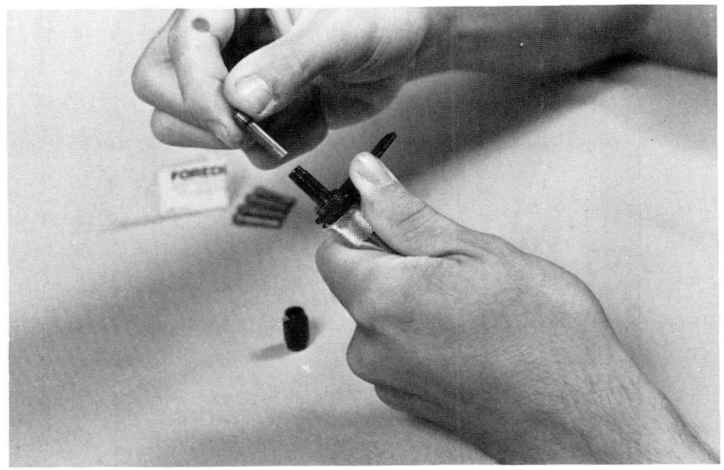

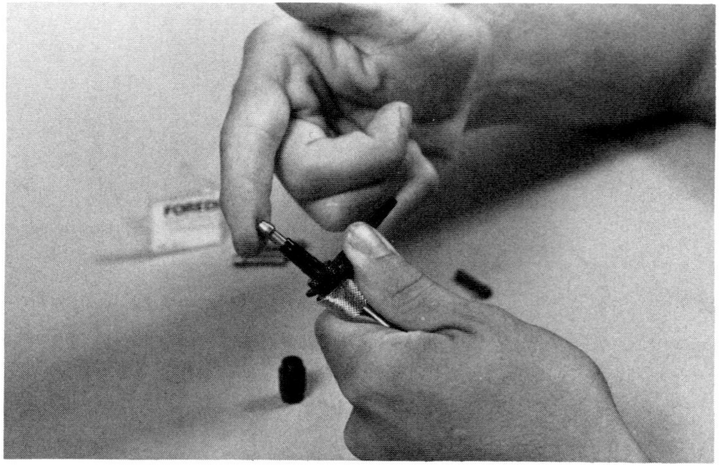

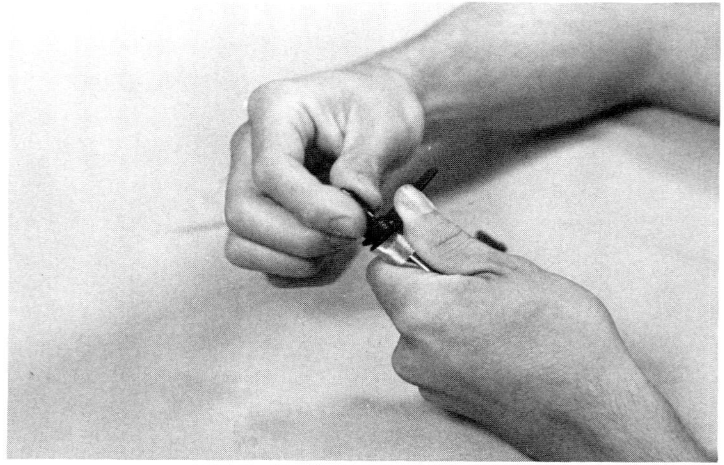

Example—series of steps in setting a particular bit in the above listed handpiece

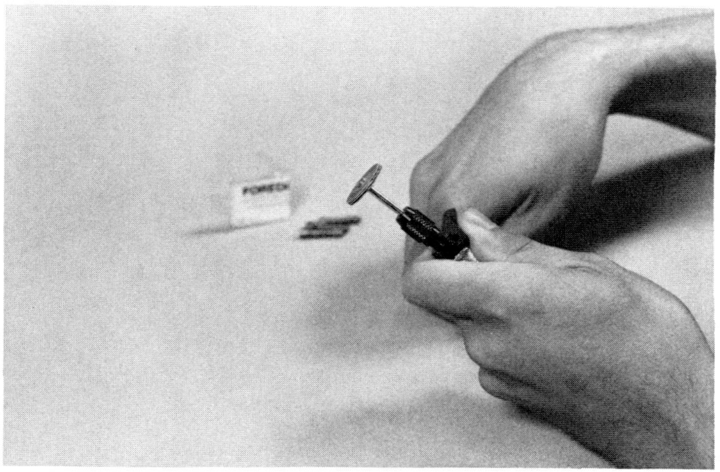

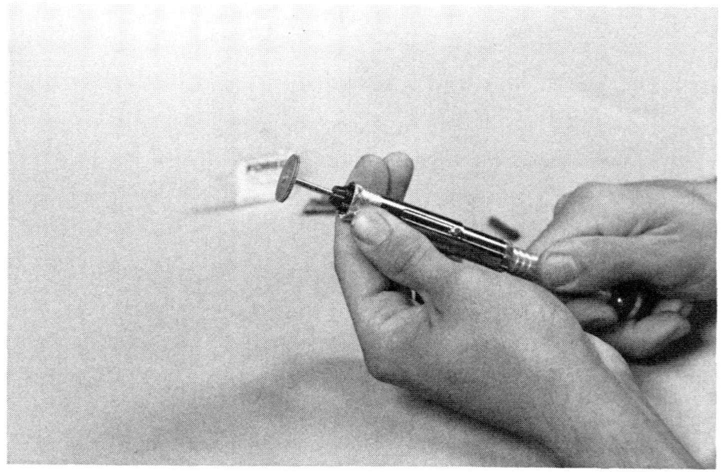

Example—steps in placing bit into a #30 greased chuck handpiece

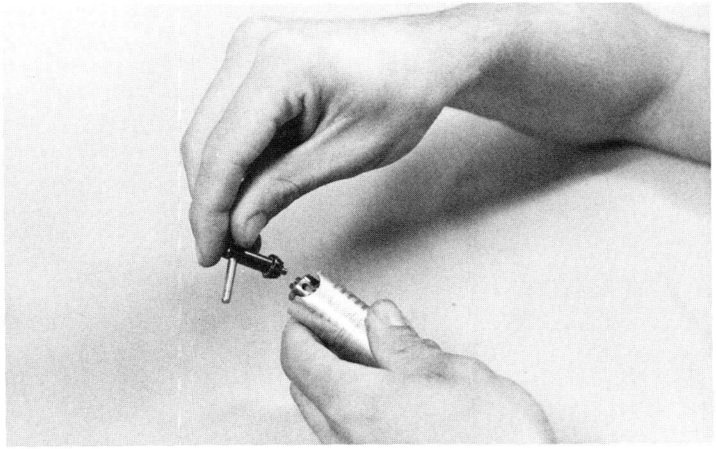

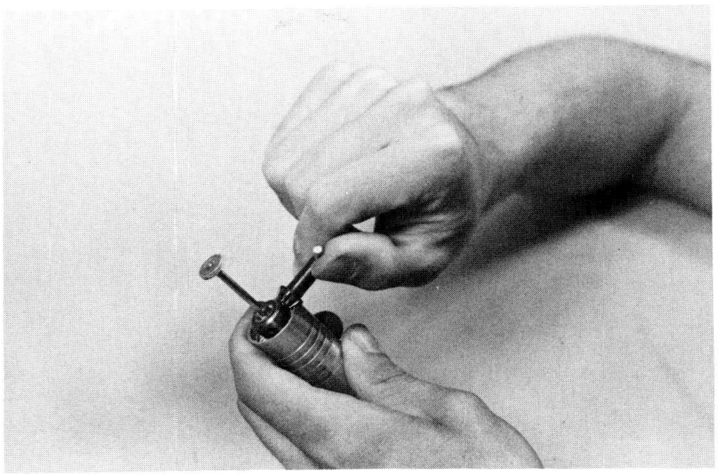

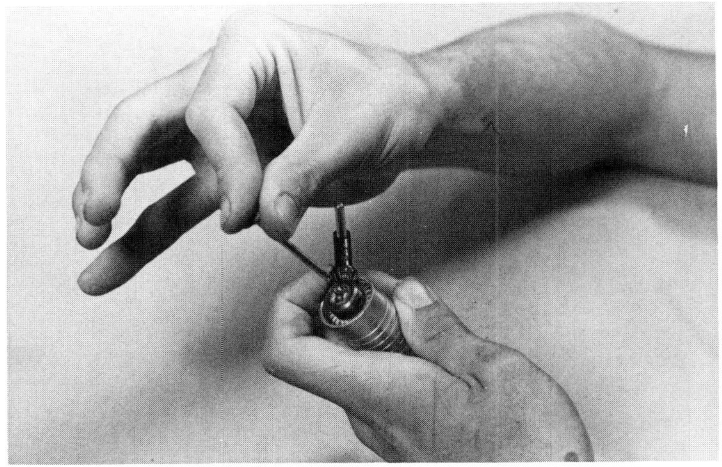

Example—tightening chuck of 44B handpiece

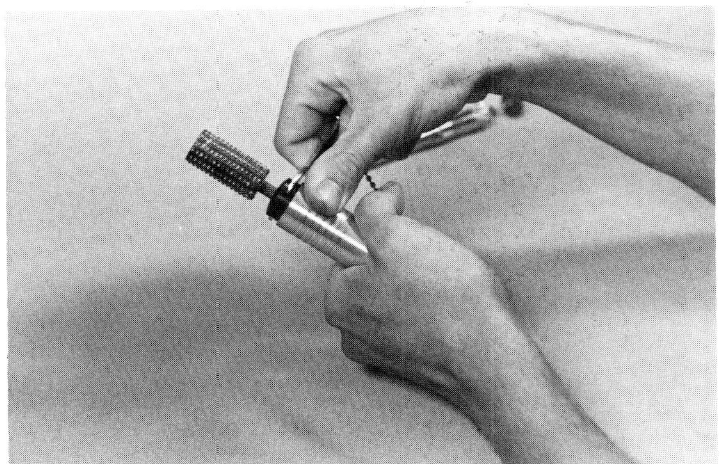

Example—series of steps to attach handpiece to flexable shaft. There is a tiny ball secured by a snap-ring—the ball snaps into groove at end of sheath and is securely held there. To disengage simply hold handpiece in one hand—sheath in the other hand and pull.

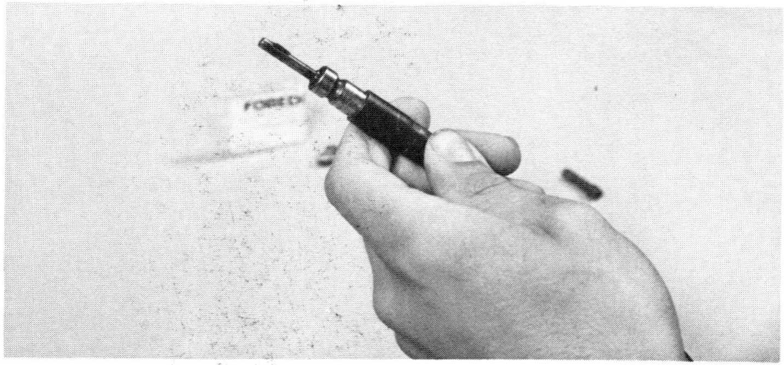

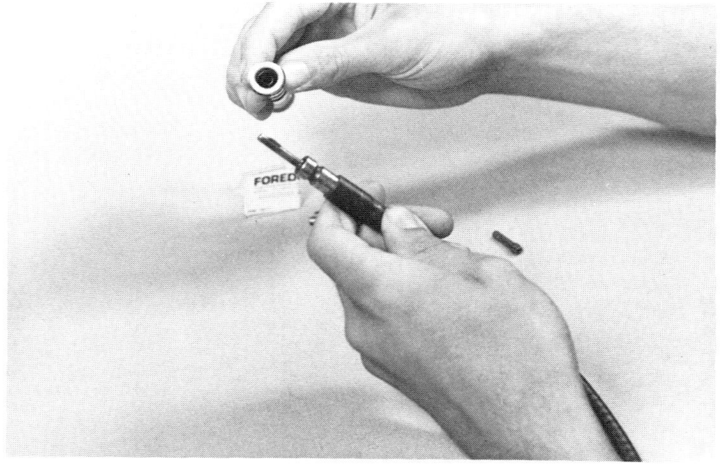

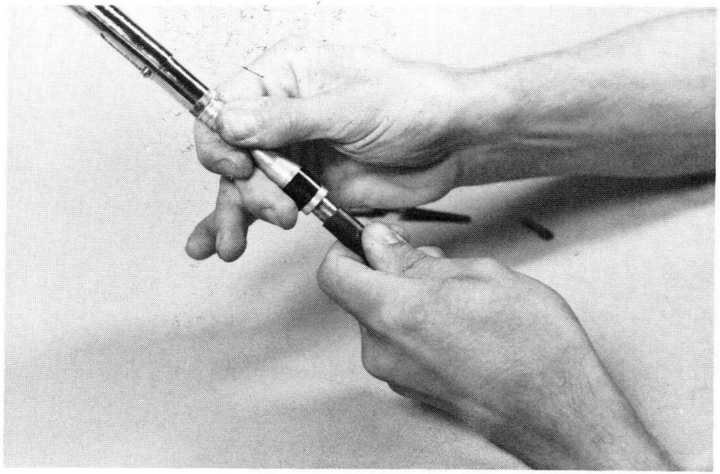

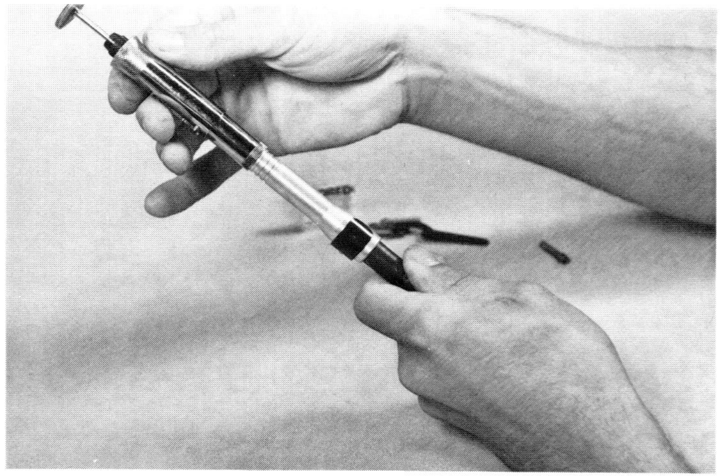

Example—series of steps to set bit in 44B handpiece as well as changing collet for different shank sizes of bits. To lock handpiece, align hole in handpiece with one on interior shaft and slide pin (there is a wrench and pin on chain provided with handpiece) through to lock—then insert bit into head and firmly tighten with wrench. Do not overtighten

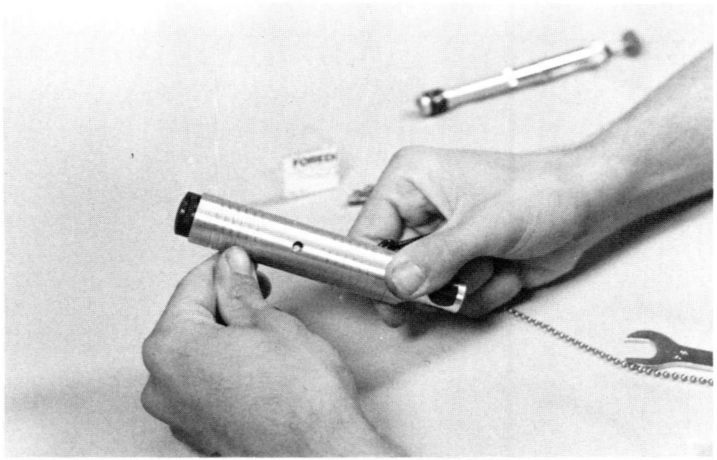

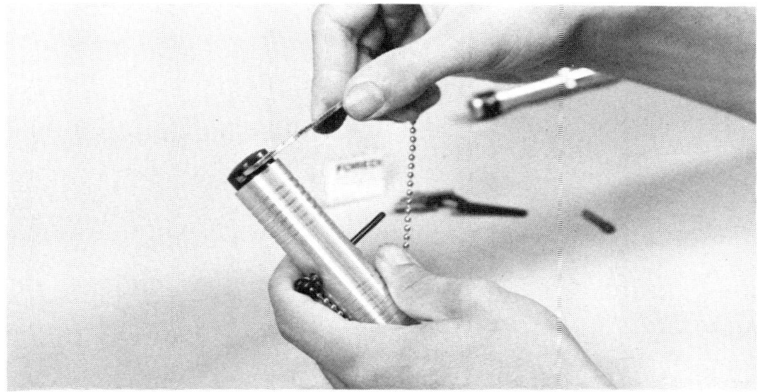

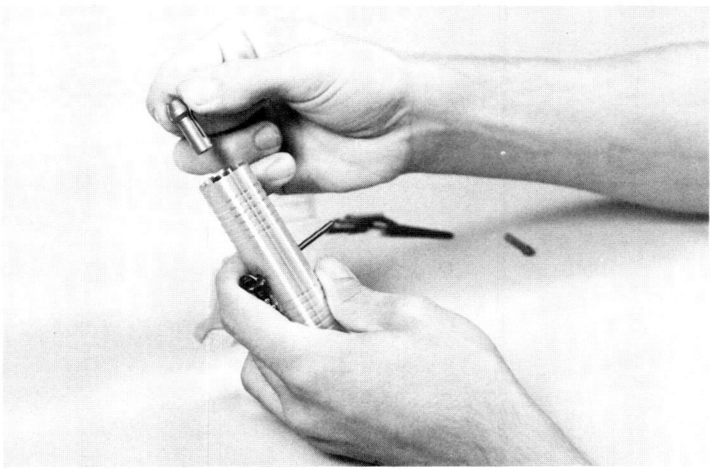

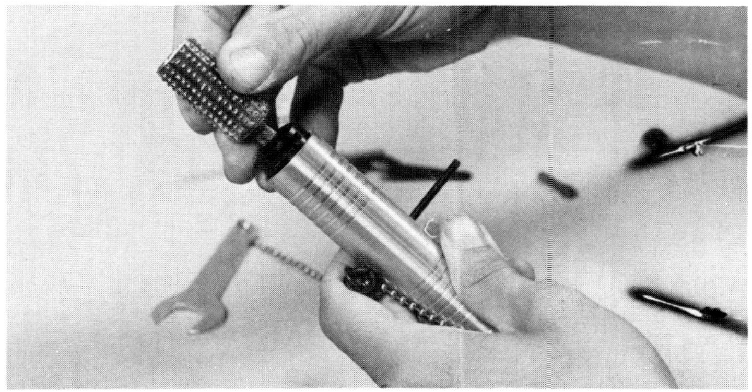

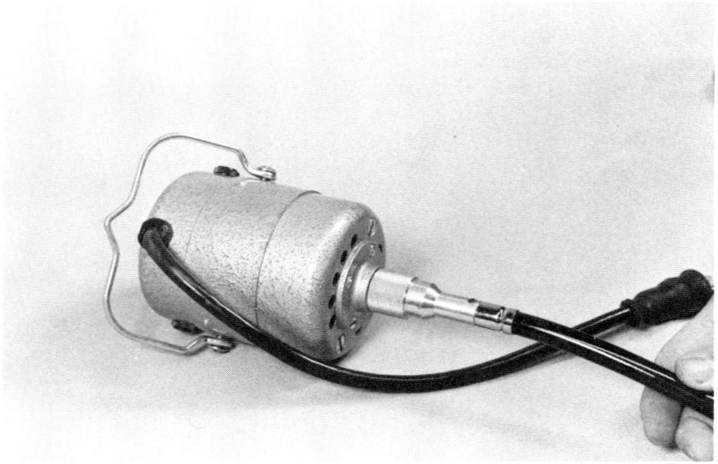

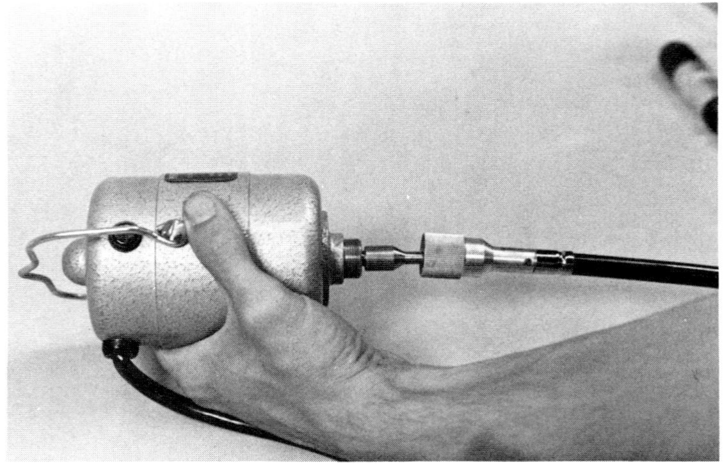

Example—changing shaft and sheath on Pfingst machine
(Cyclone would be the same) same procedure as Foredom

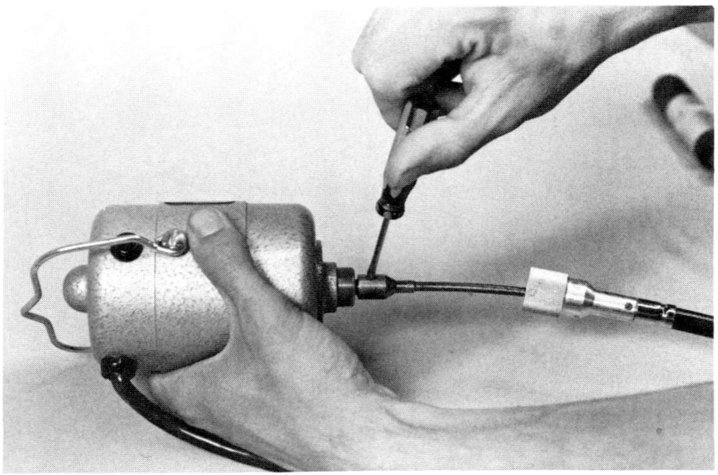

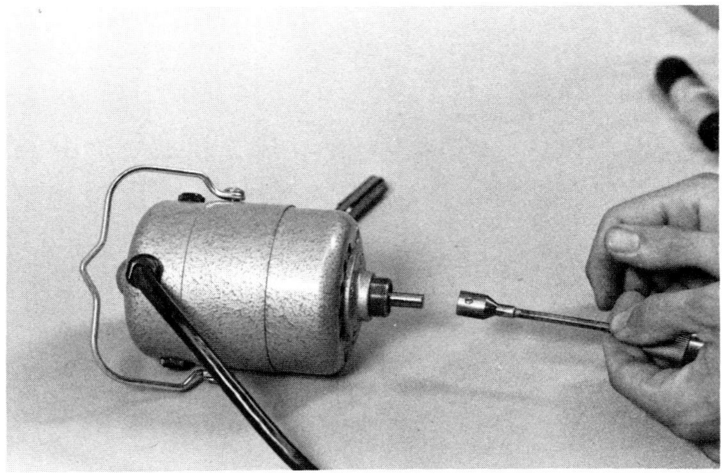

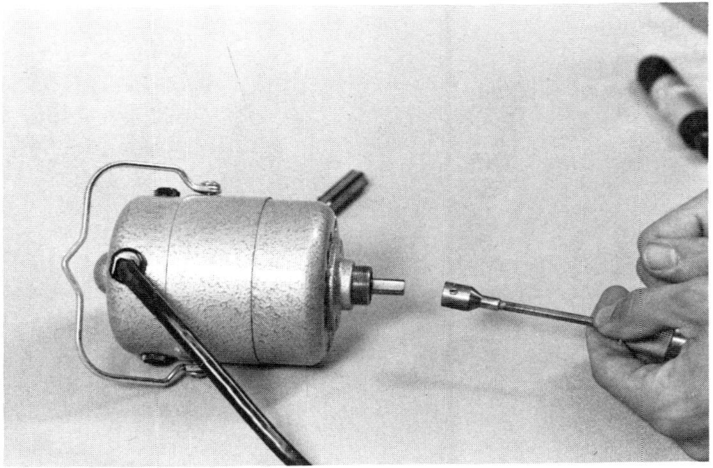

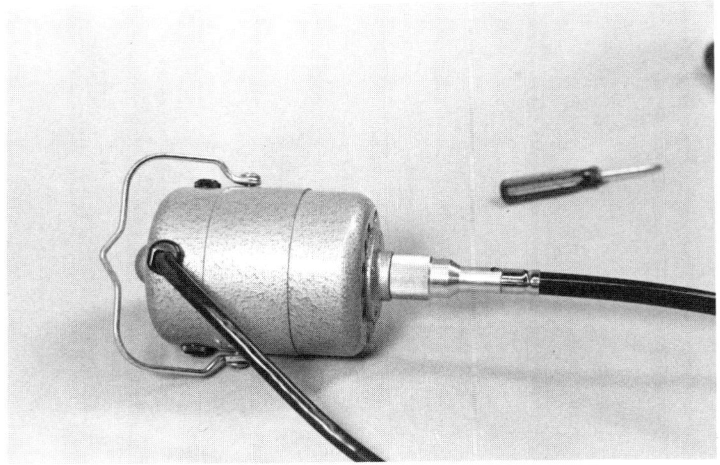

Example—adjusting shaft and sheath on Pfingst machine
(Cyclone same) same procedure as Foredom

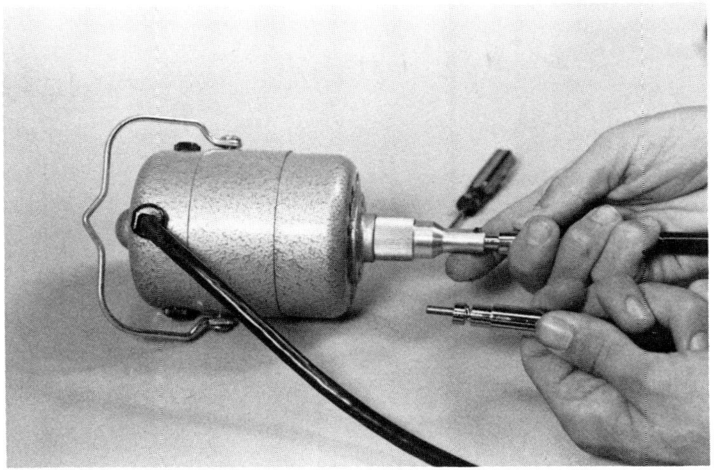

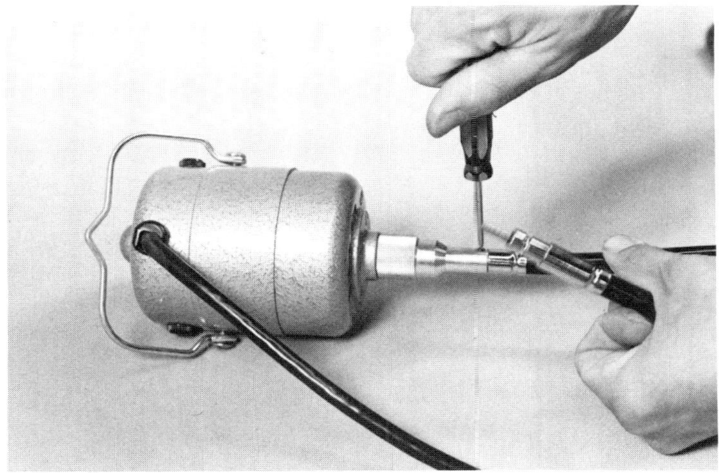

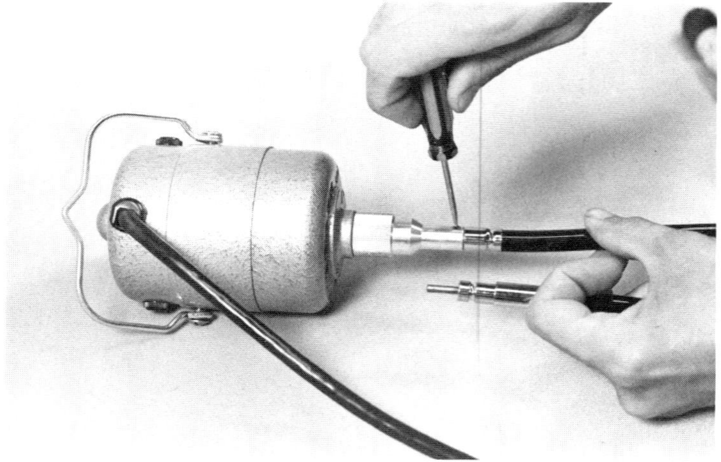

Adjusting sheath on Pfingst machine

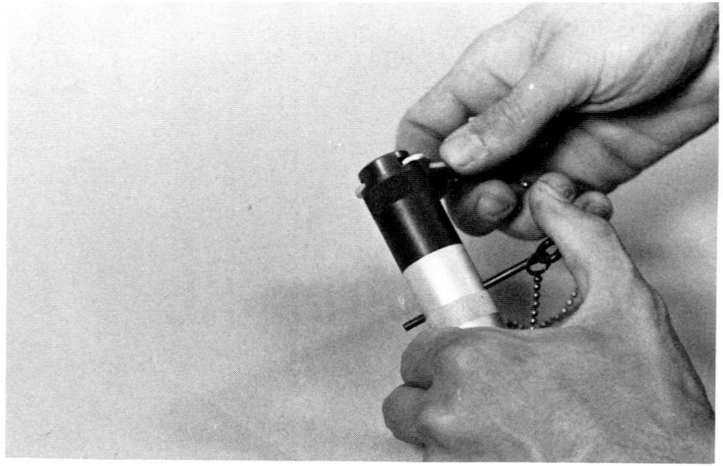

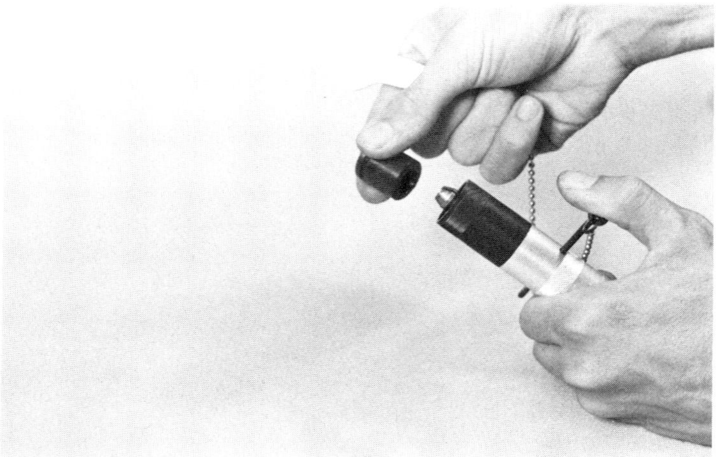

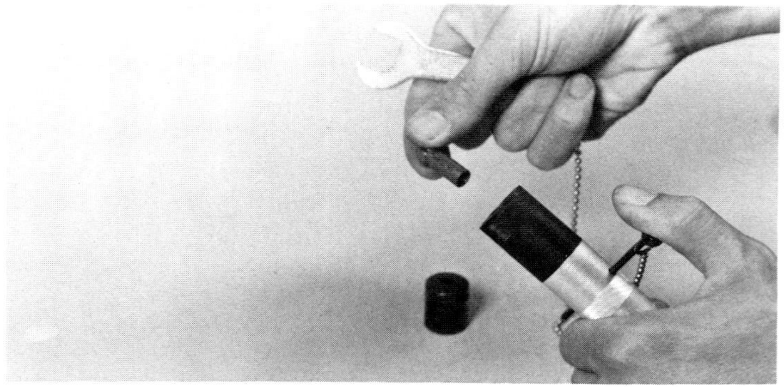

Example—series of steps changing collets in Pfingst 44B equivalent handpiece

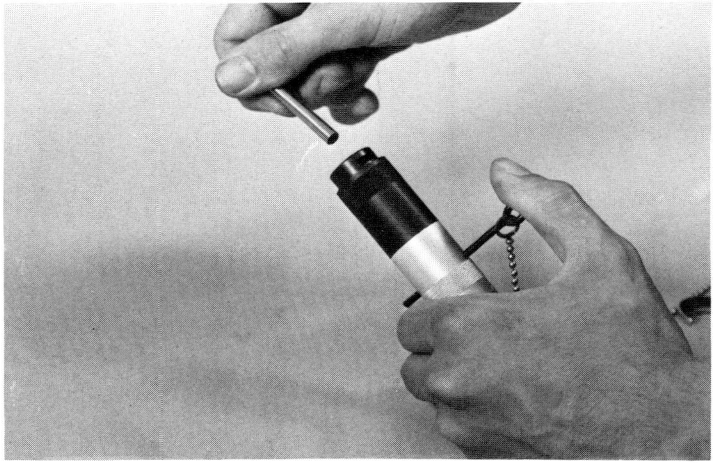
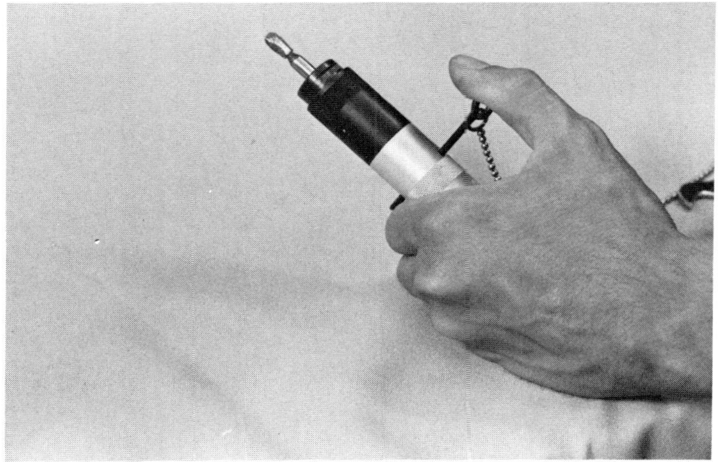

Example—setting bits and handpieces in Pfingst machine similar to Foredom and Cyclone

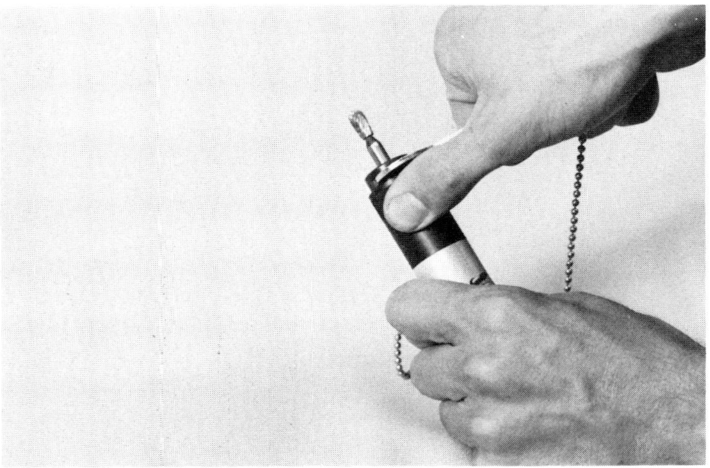
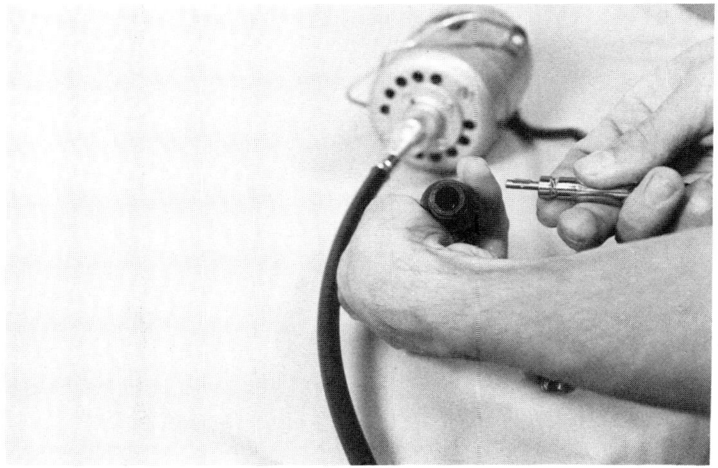

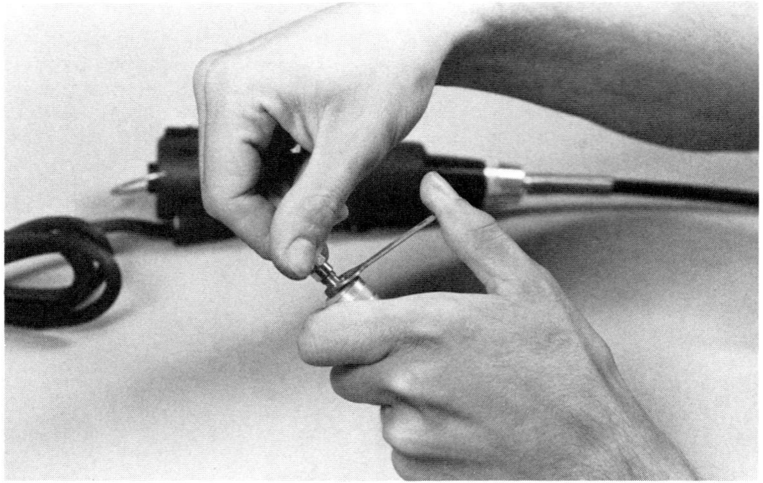

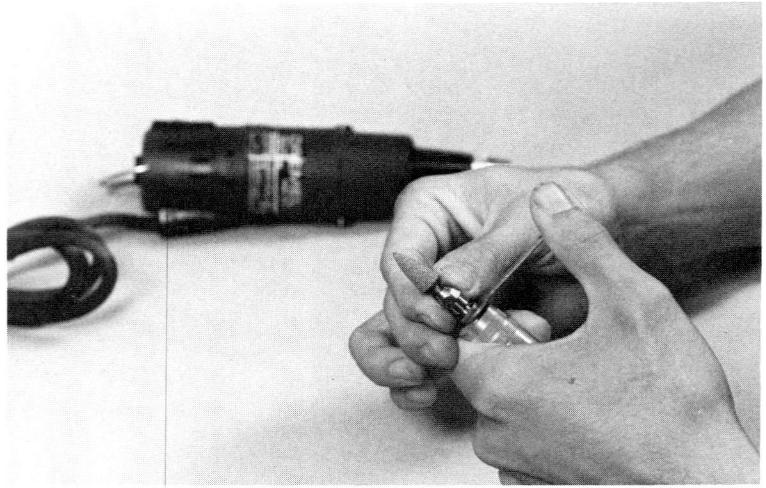

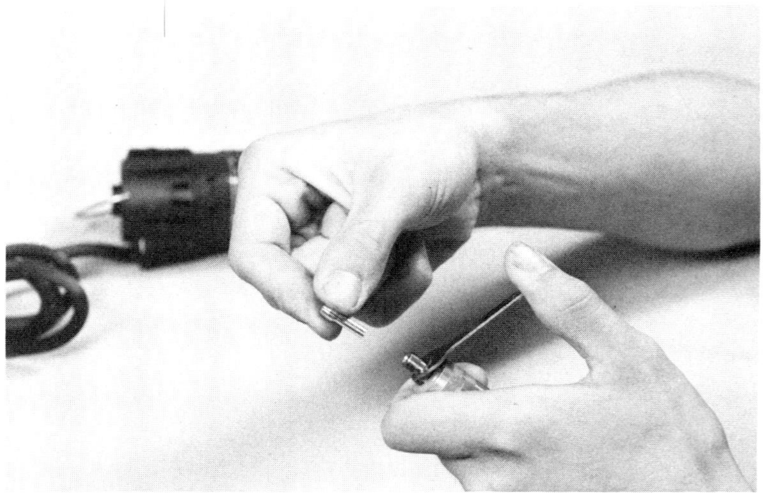

Example—steps in setting bits in Dremel handpiece

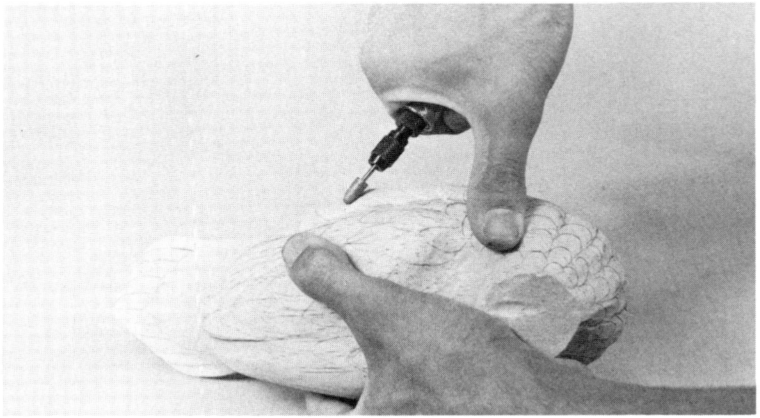

Example—ruby carver with #8 handpiece outlining in feather group as first steps in creating roundness (fluffiness) in feathers

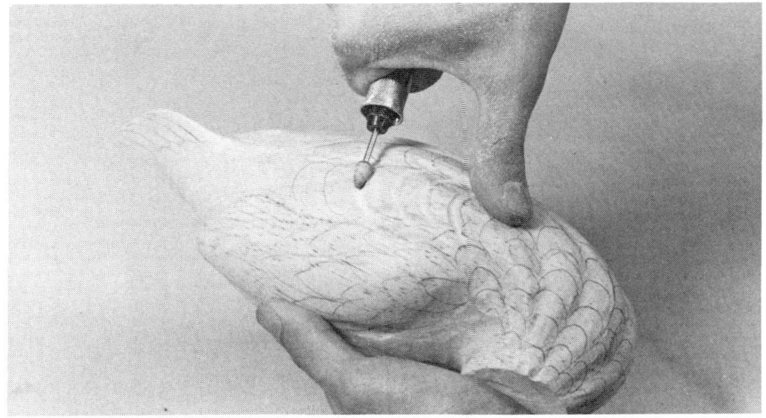

Example—final shaping with ruby carver

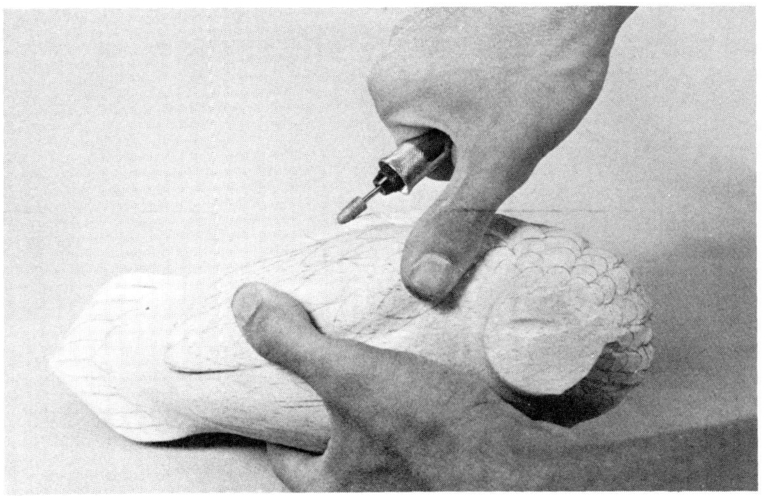

Example—smoothing each feather with ruby carver

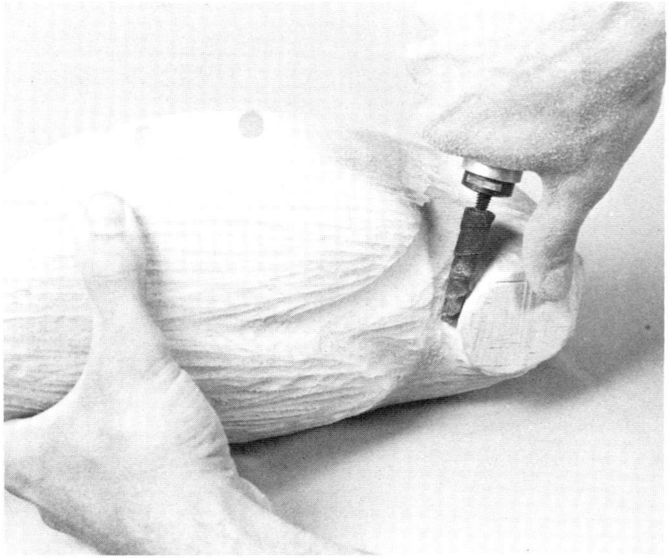

Example—sanding tight areas with tapered sanding cartridge

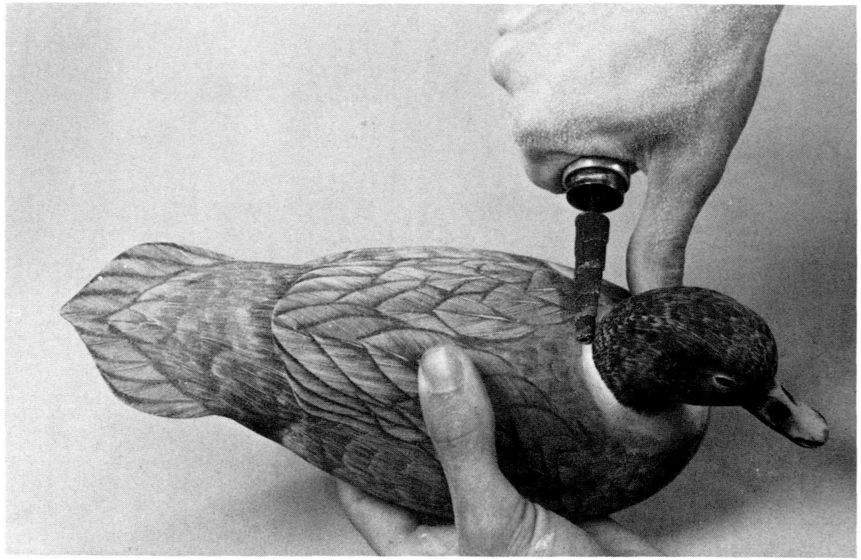

Example—sanding neck joint with tapered sanding cartridge

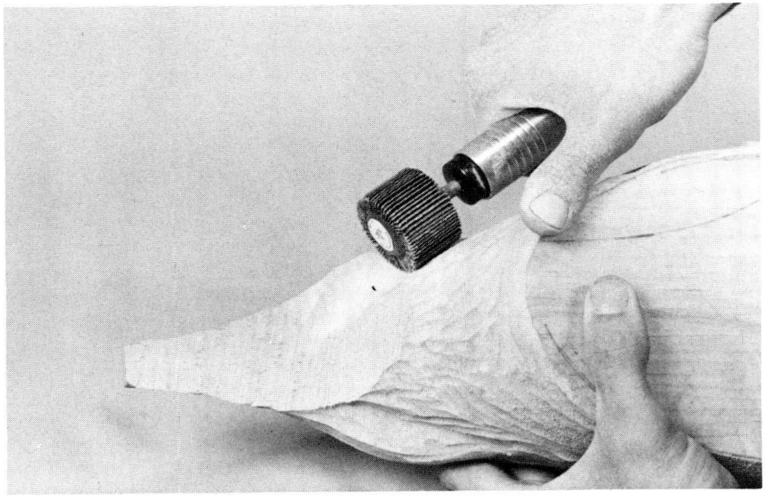

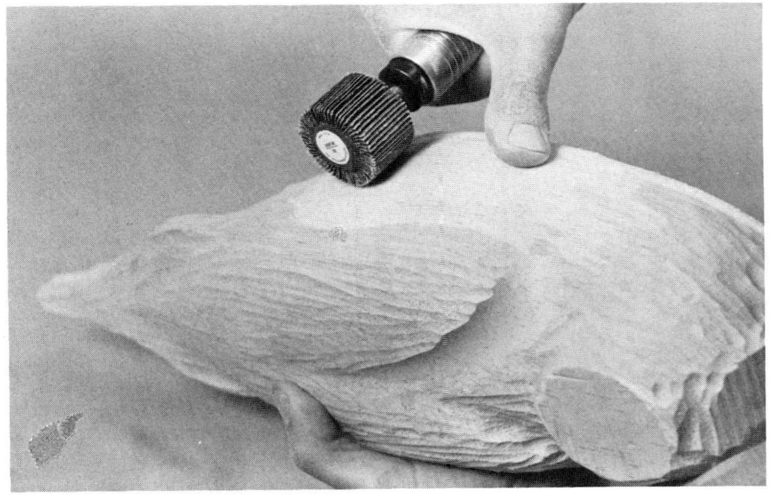

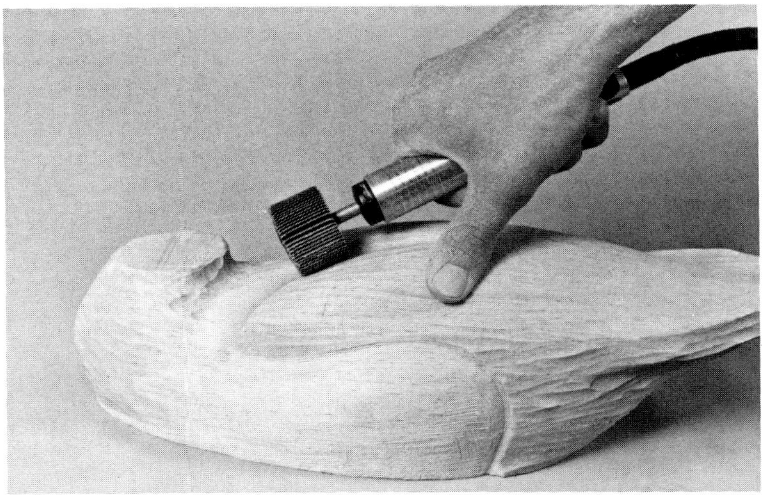

Series of examples of rough sanding with 1" or 2" flap sander—1/4 shank using 44B handpiece. Note: anchoring of thumb to add stability.

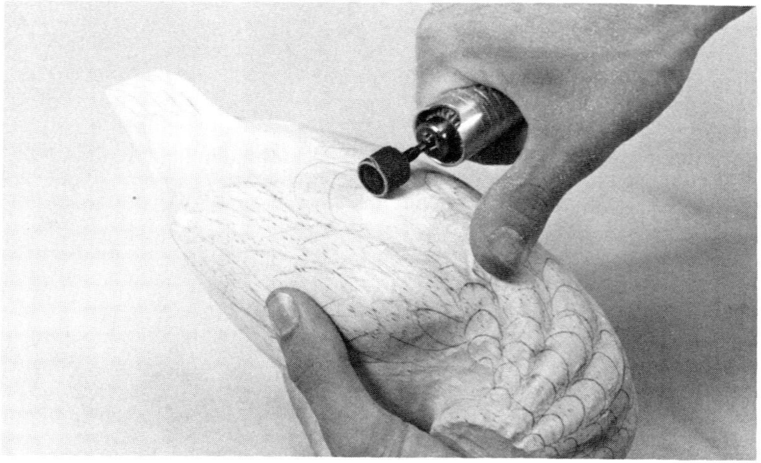

Example—sanding feather with small expandable drum sander

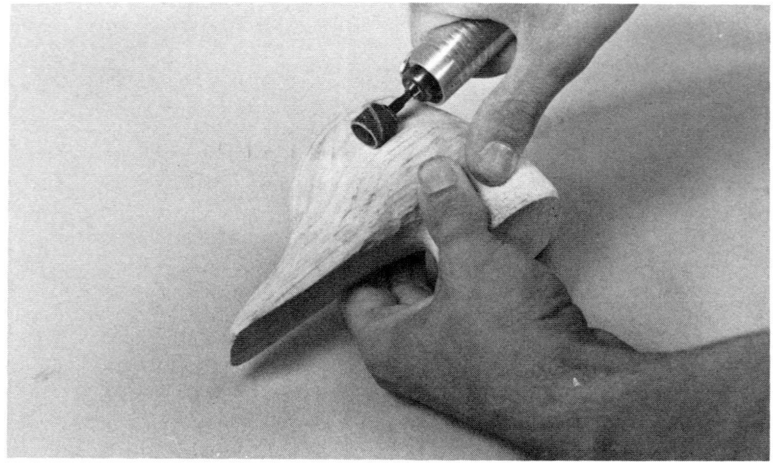

Example—sanding head with small expandable drum sander

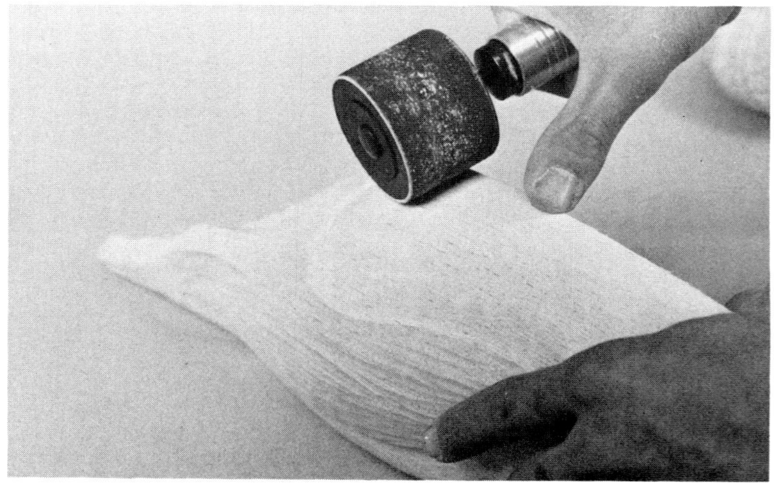

Example—rough sanding with large expandable drum sander

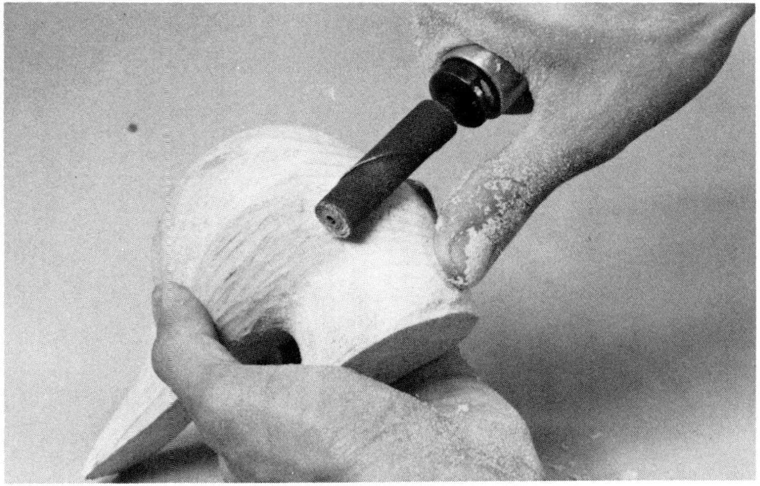

Example—sanding back of head with round cartridge roll (tootsie roll)

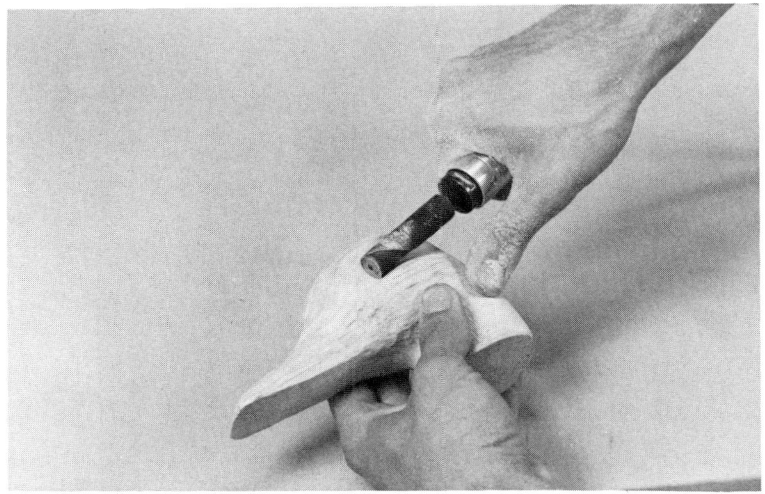

Example—sanding eye channel with round cartridge roll

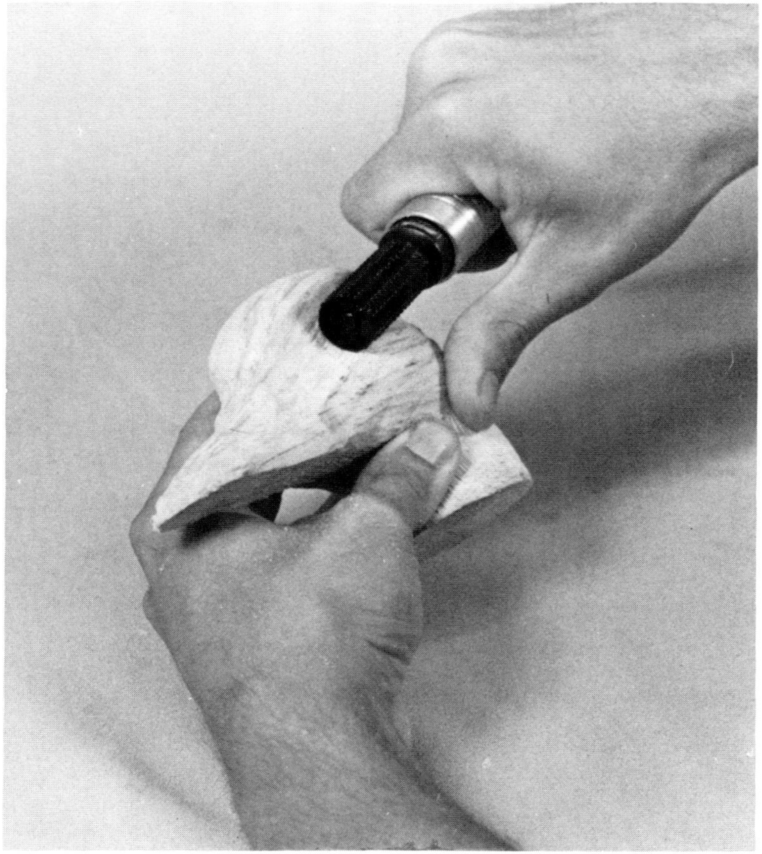

Example—carving eye channel with 3/4" hollow Arco rasp

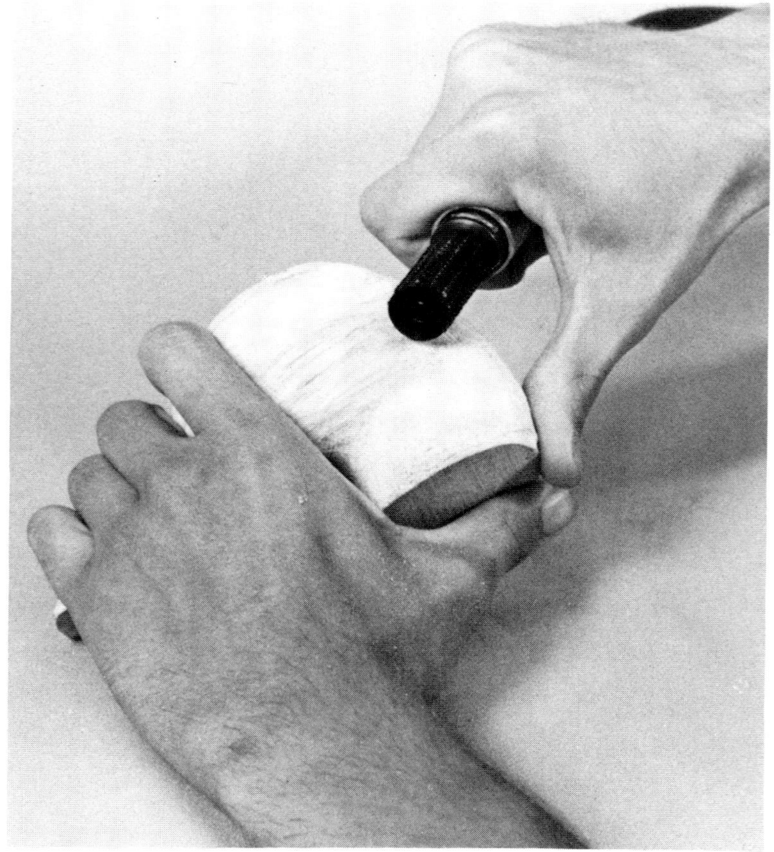

Example—carving back of head with 3/4" hollow Arco rasp

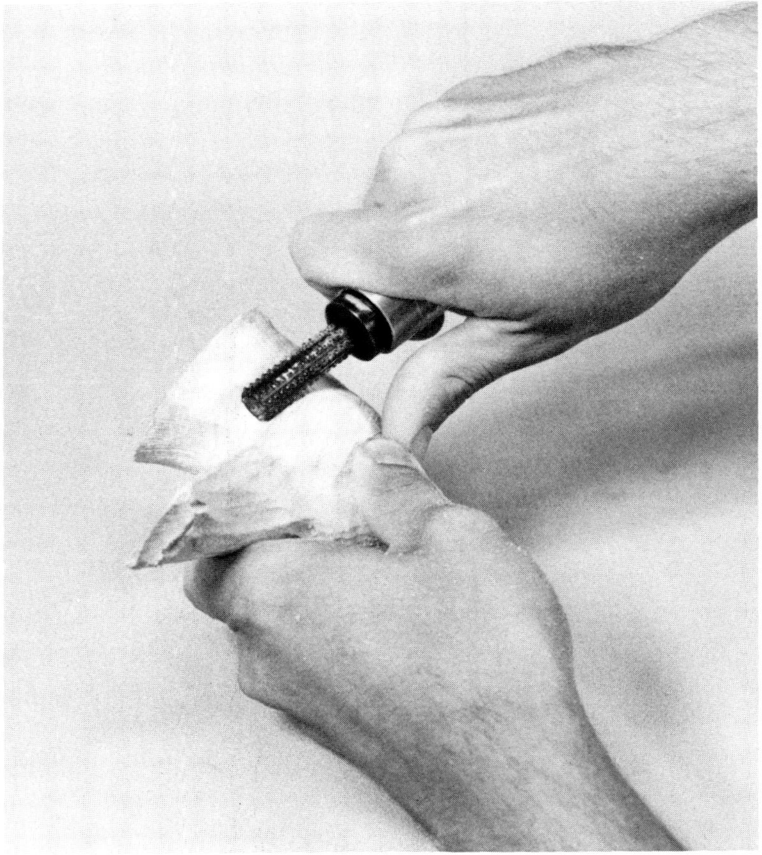

Example—carving throat (under cheek) with 1/2" Arco hollow rasp

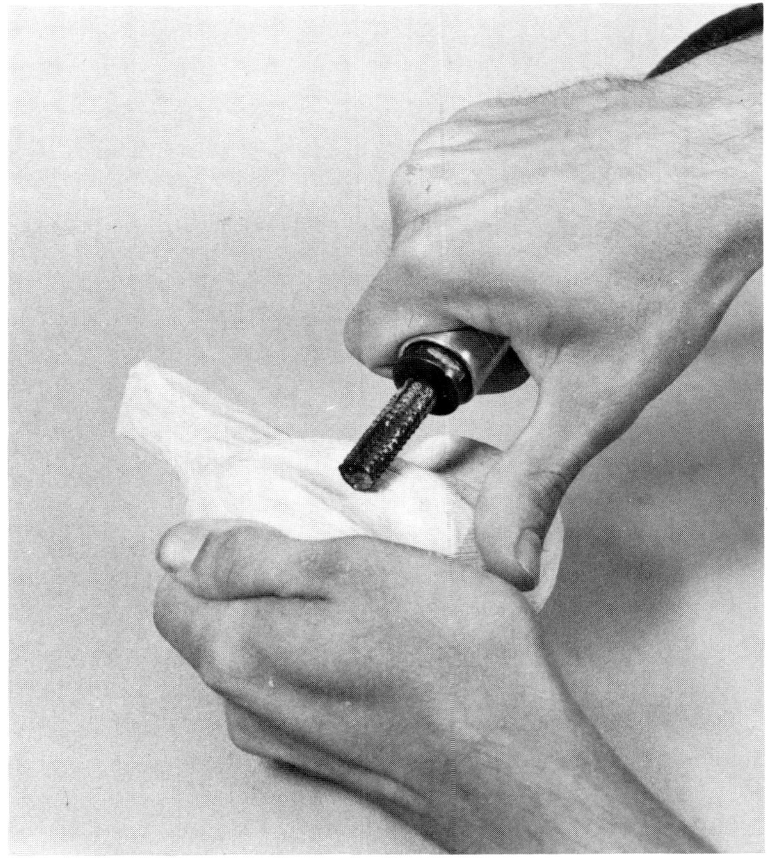

Example—shaping cheek area with 1/2" Arco hollow rasp

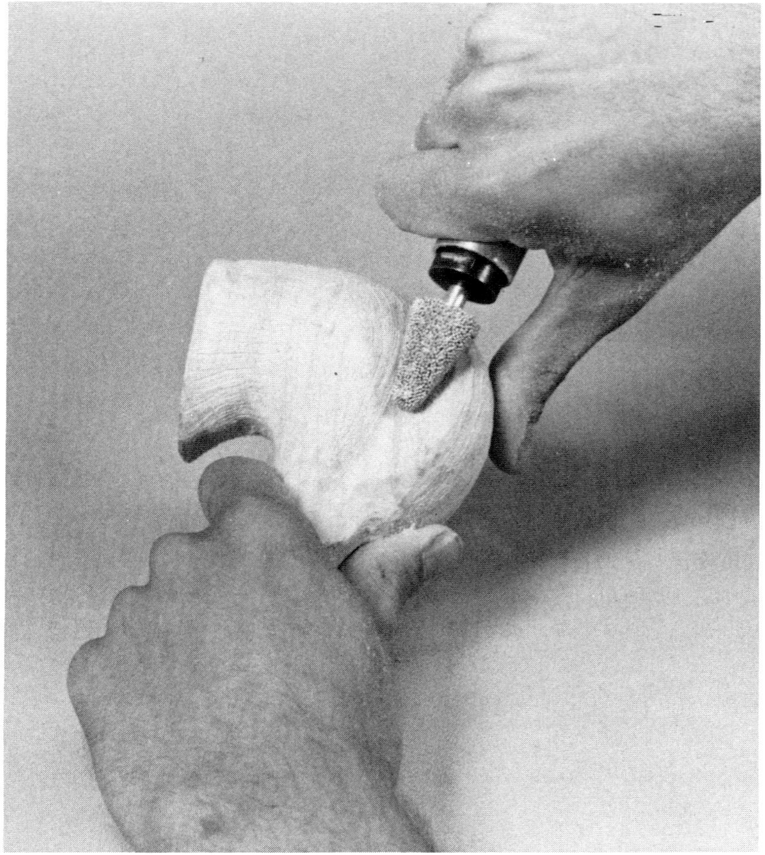

Example—shaping eye channel with 3/4'' Karbide Kutzall

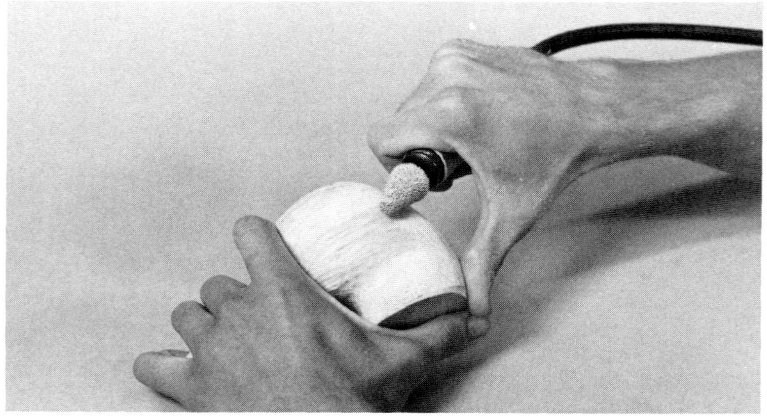

Example—shaping back of head with 3/4'' Karbide Kutzall

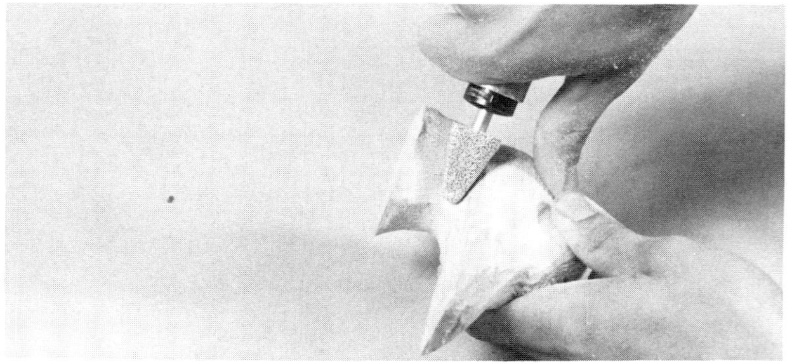

Example—shaping under cheek and throat with 3/4'' Karbide Kutzall

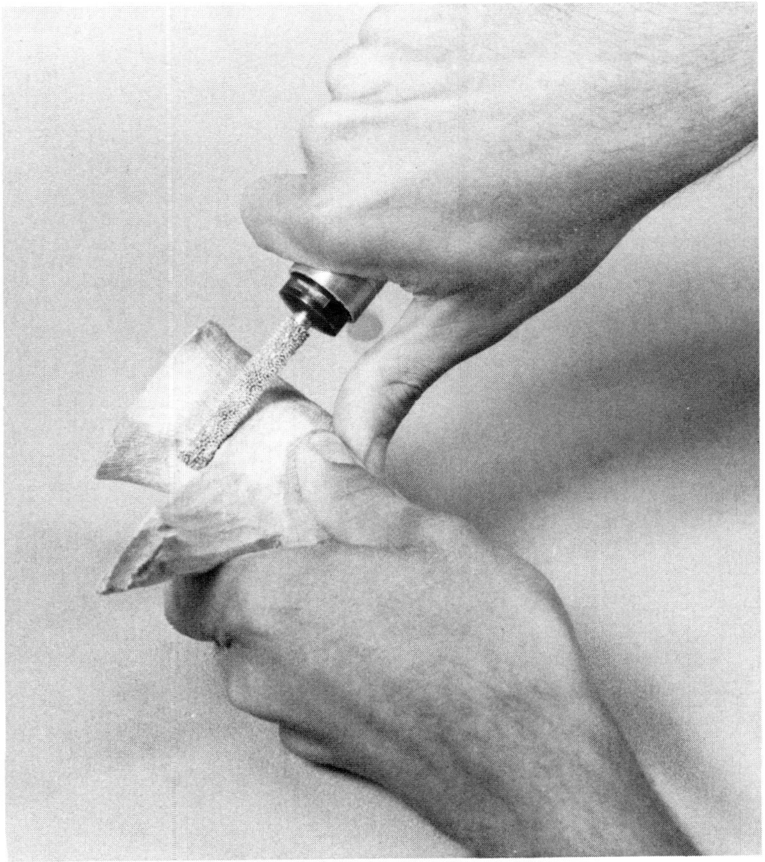

Example—shaping small radius with 1/2" cyclinder Karbide Kutzall

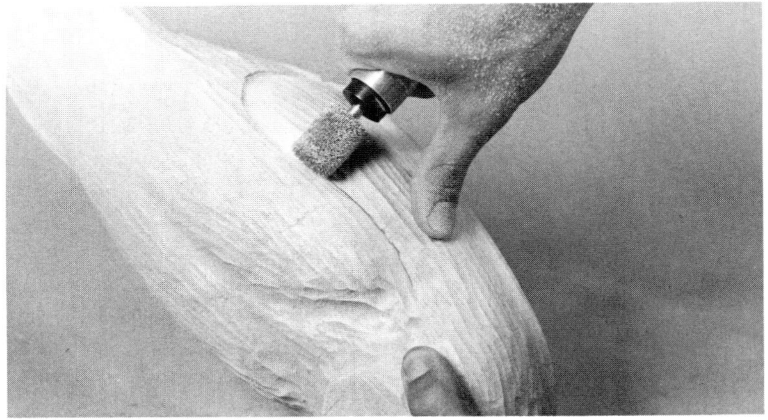

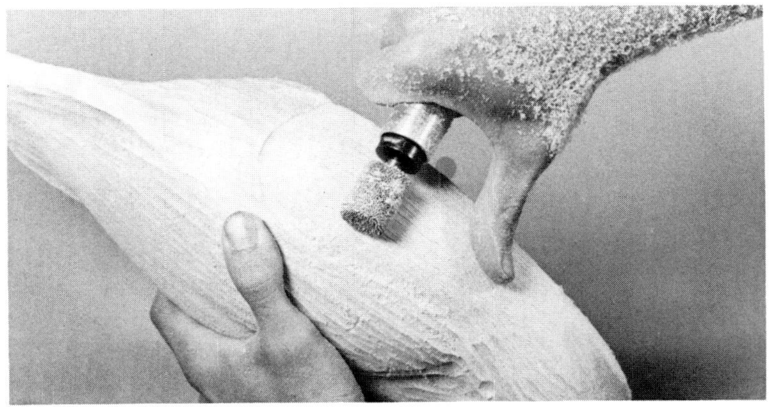

Example—shaping broad areas with 1" Karbide Kutzall

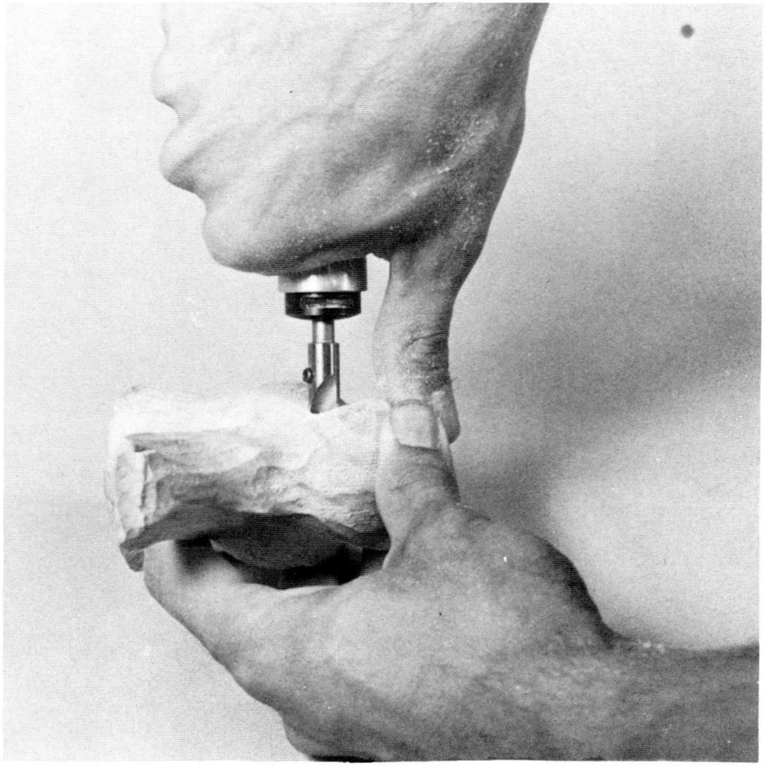

Example—different bits for eye drilling (many carvers use tiny ruby bits to carve eye hole just barely large enough to insert eye, this includes carving eye lid and all detail, however, most just drill eye hole slightly larger than intended eye and fill with moldable epoxy or other material and shape to desired shape.

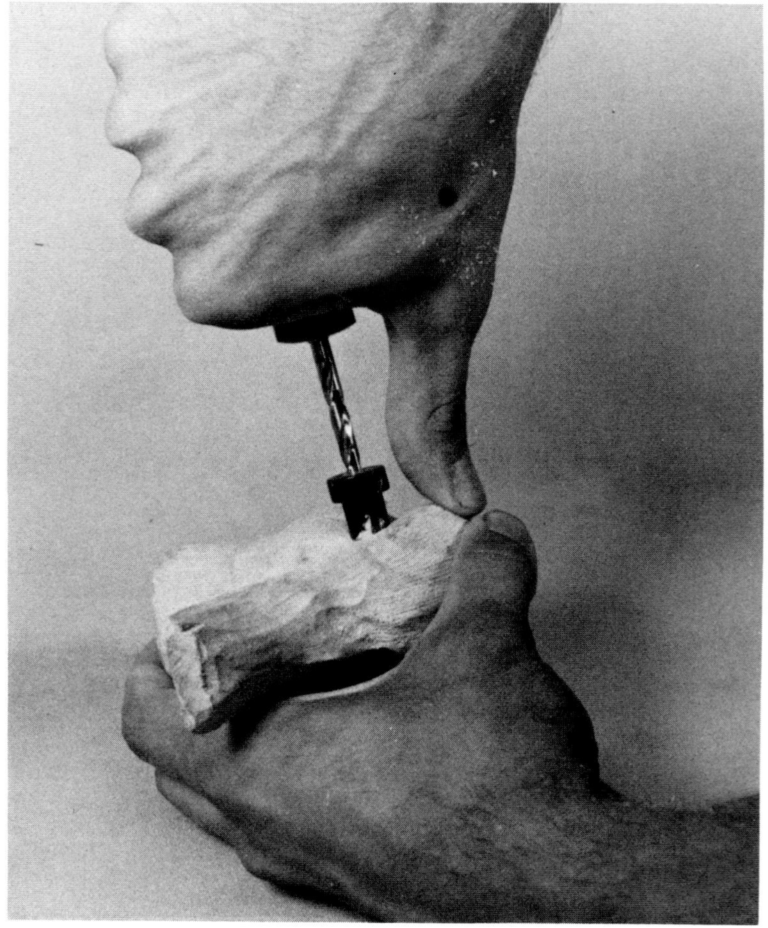

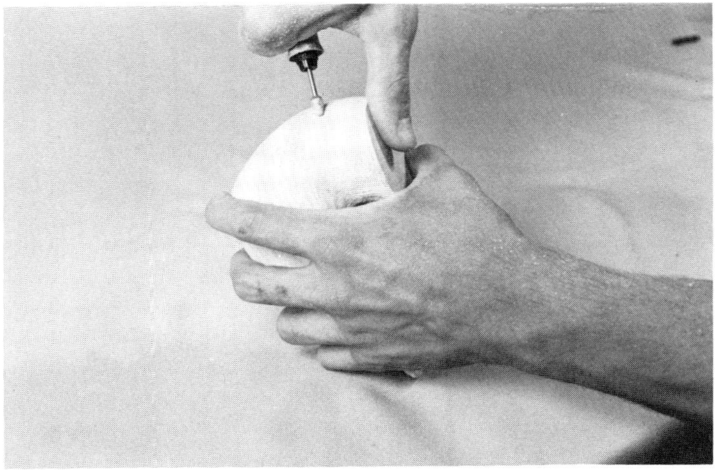

Example—shaping with small ruby carver

Example—texturing with stone using #8 handpiece

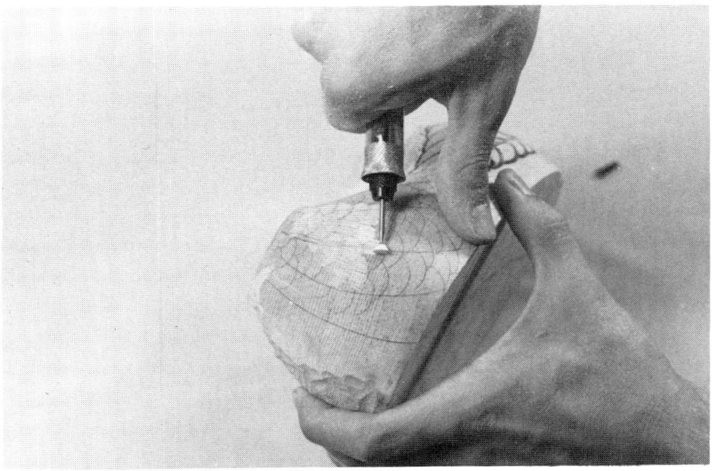

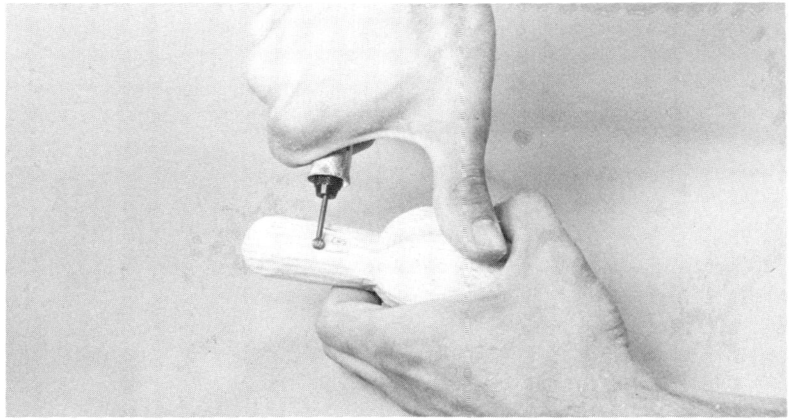

Example—detailing upper mandible using small burr and #8 handpiece

Example—using small burr and #8 handpiece to hollow bill for open bill. Lower mandible will be carved and inserted.

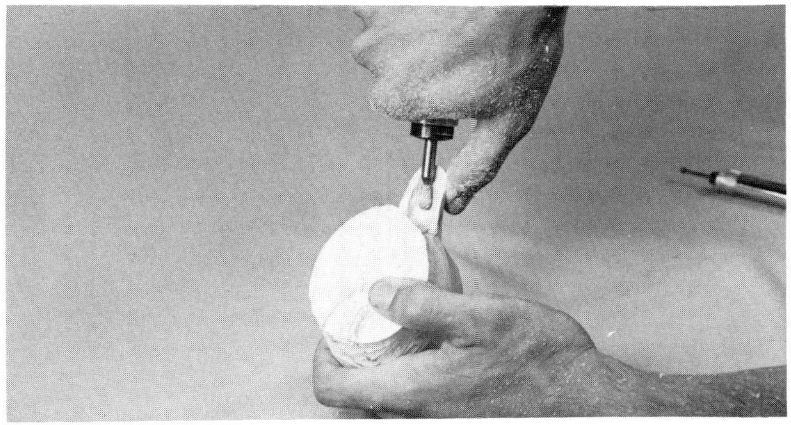

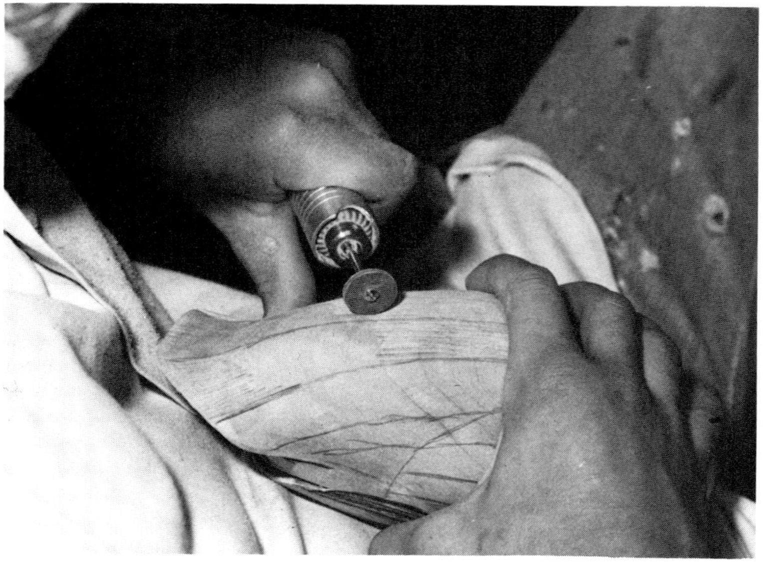

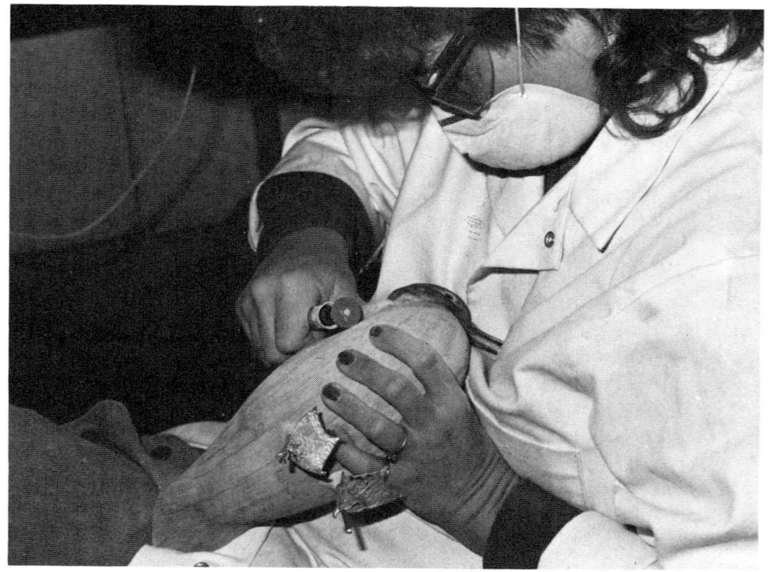

Example—detailing by using dental separating discs—use two or more discs with a broken one as a spacer. These discs are brittle so always be certain to use eye protection, they can shatter.

Example—of texturing feather pattern with dental discs

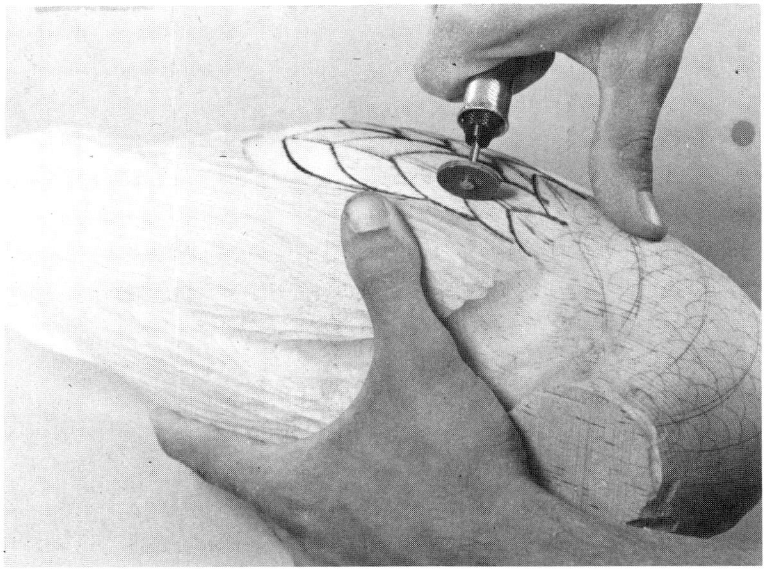

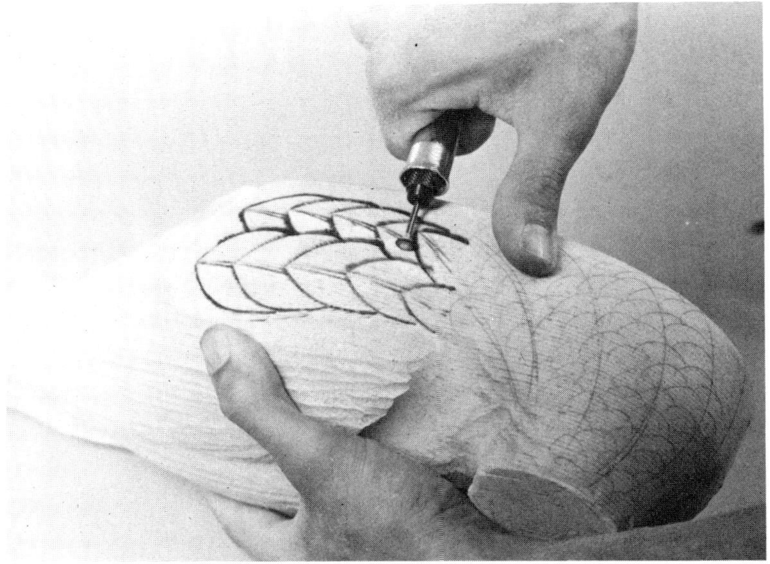

Example—texturing feather pattern using small stone

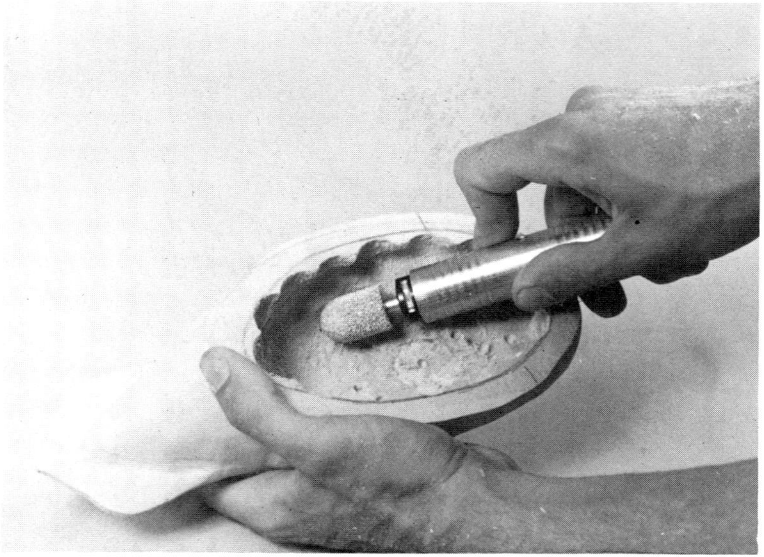

Example—hollowing with 1'' ball nose Karbide Kutzall

Example—hollowing with 1/2'' ball nose solid Arco rasp

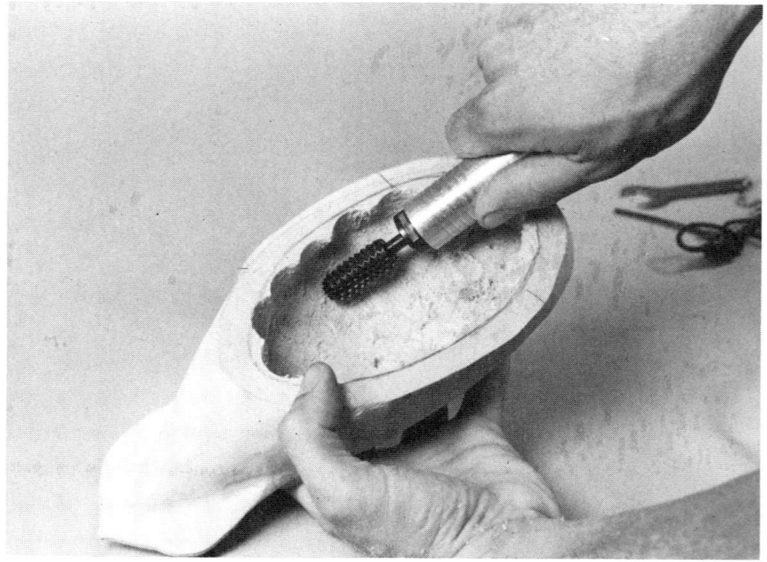

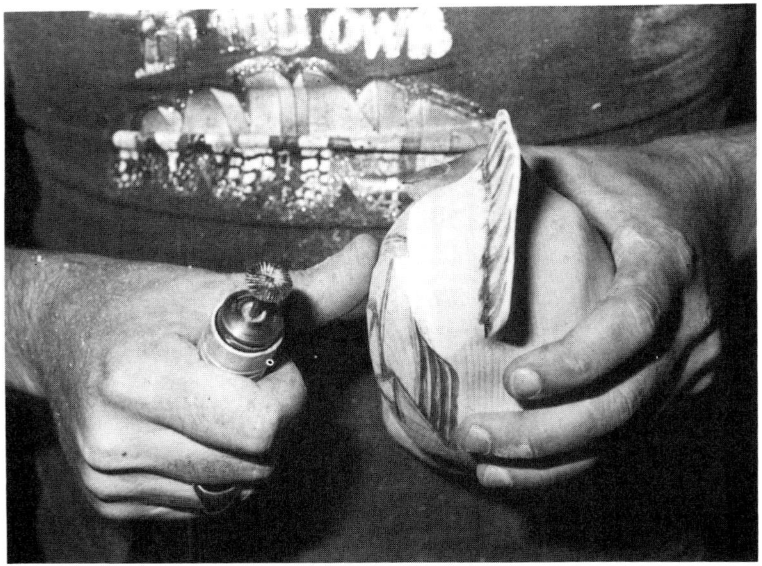

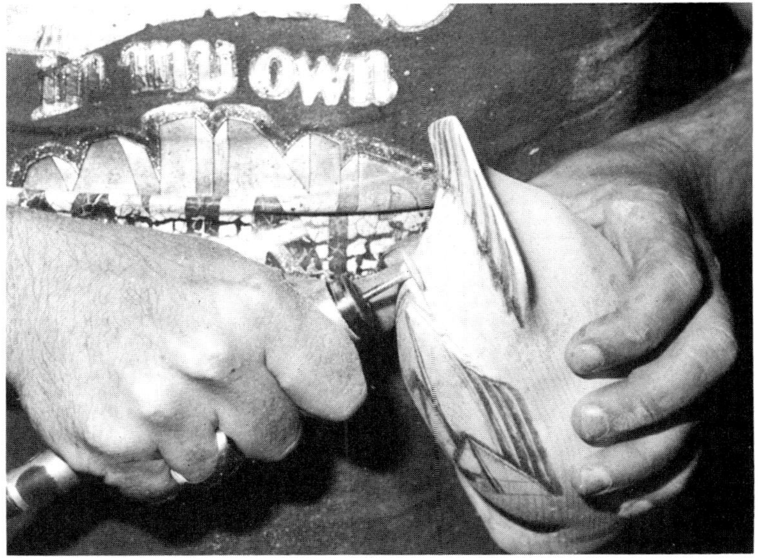

Example—cutting channel for primary inserts using small saw like bit. This is a potentially dangerous operation—*keep fingers away* from work area and avoid distractions

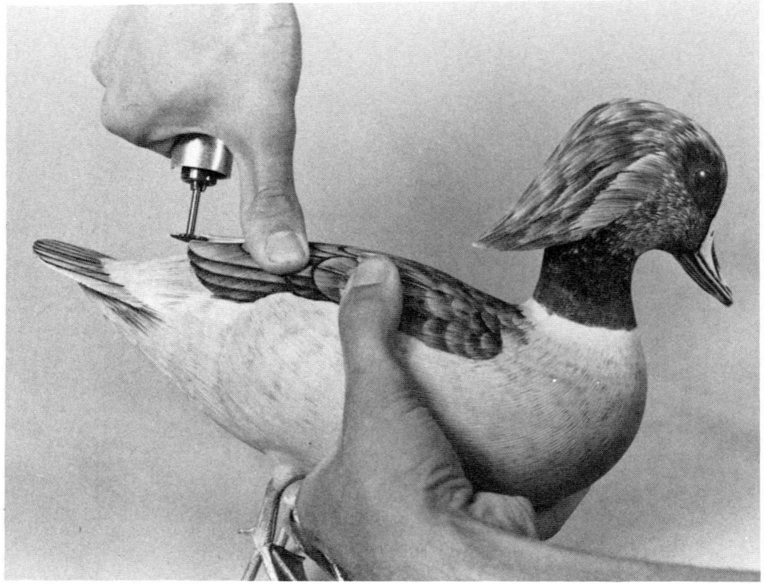

Channel—be firm but cautious so as not to overcut

Further examples of cutting

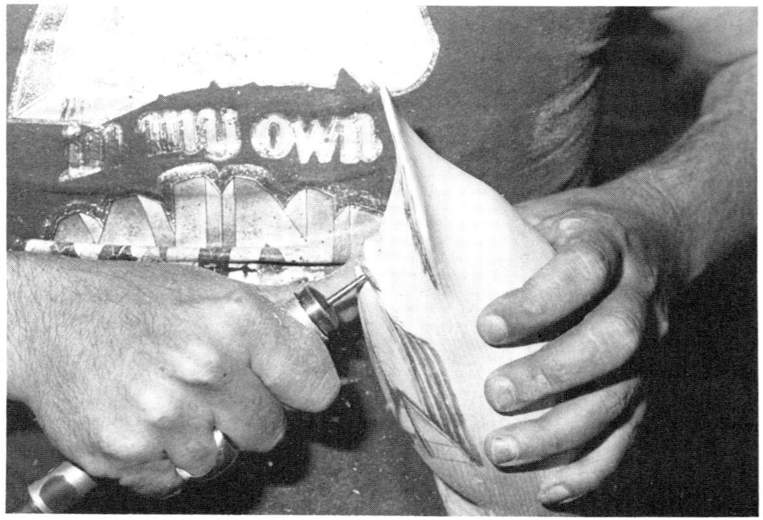

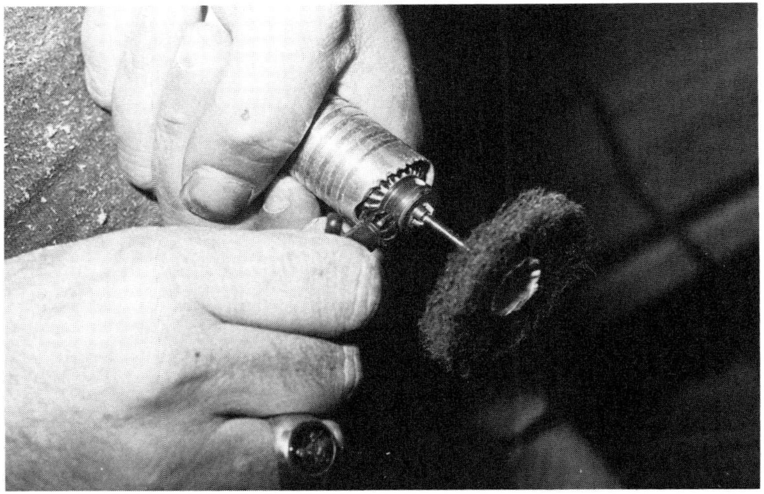

Disc of scotchbrite on mandrel with #30 handpiece

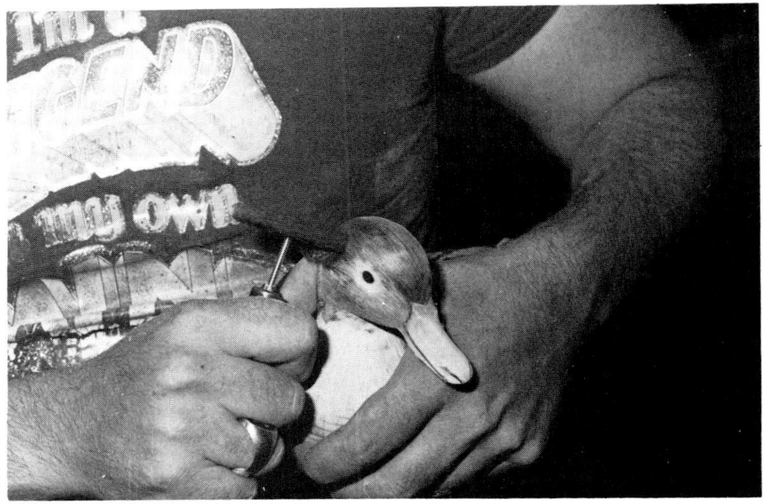

Example—using scotchbrite to clean dust and debris from carving prior to sealing for painting.

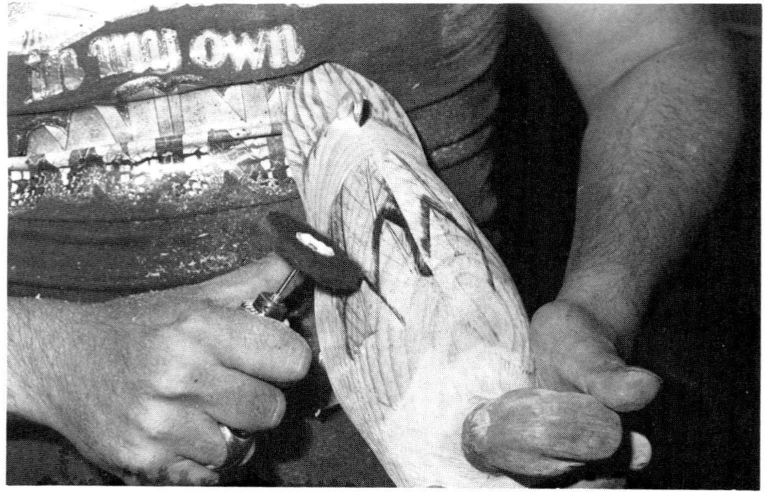

Example—left; denture brush on a mandrel used for cleaning carving. This is an excellant method, however, the bristles can tear out fill material so go gently over any area which has been filled. Above; further example of cleaning with Scotchbrite disc.

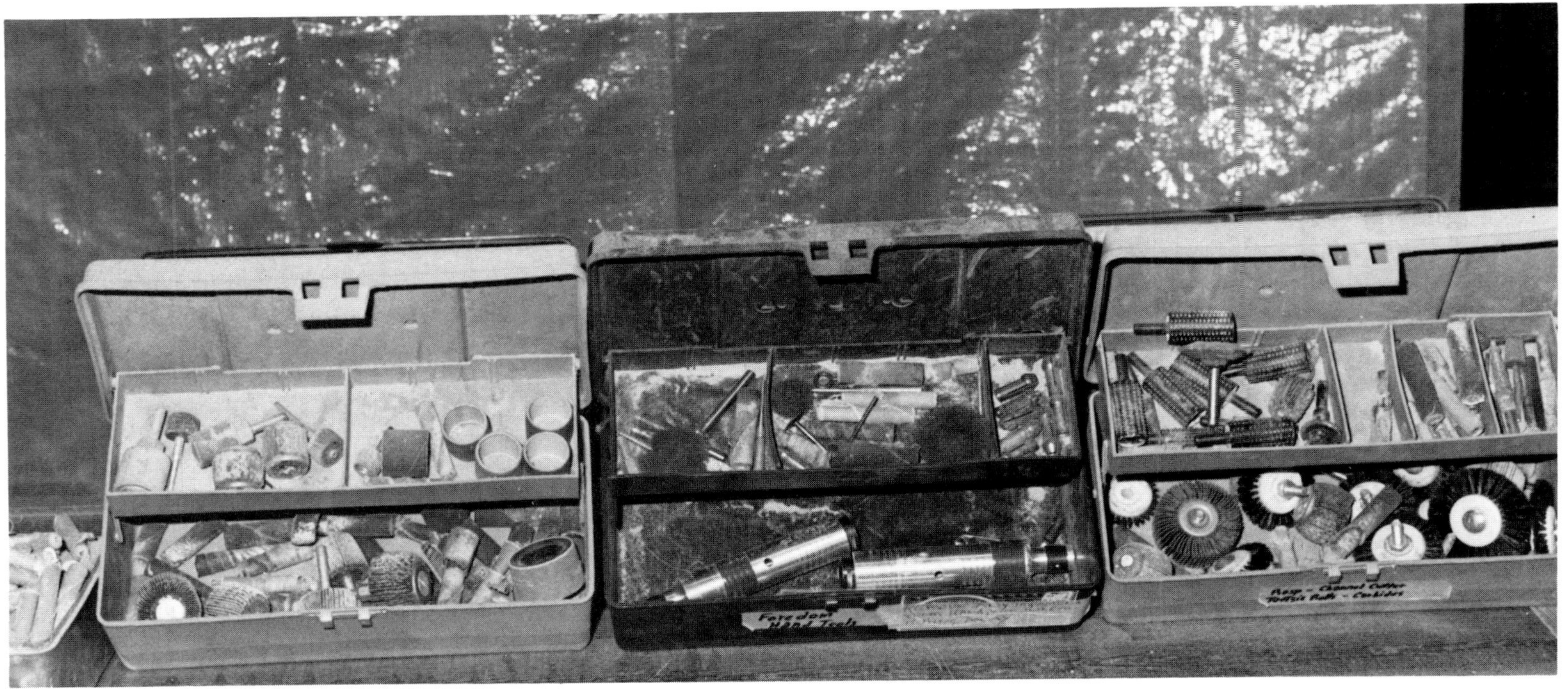

Example—tool boxes with bits

Assortment of bits and handpieces for texturing. Note: abrasive stone for sharpening

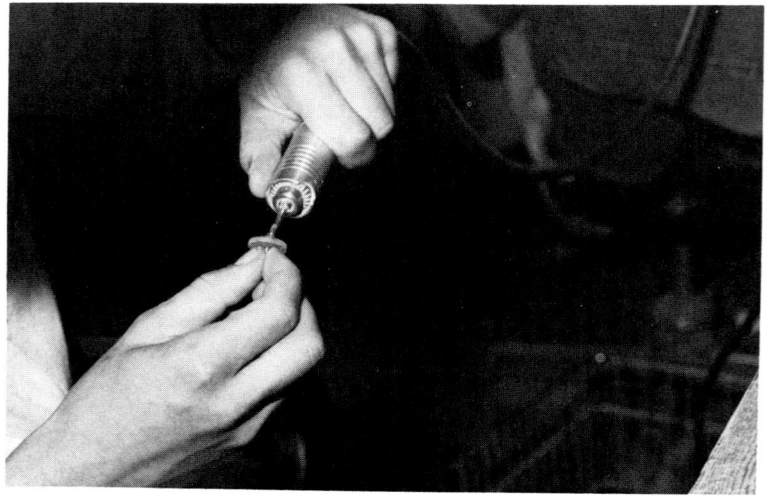

Example—replacing dental discs

Example—handpiece with discs and tootsie roll

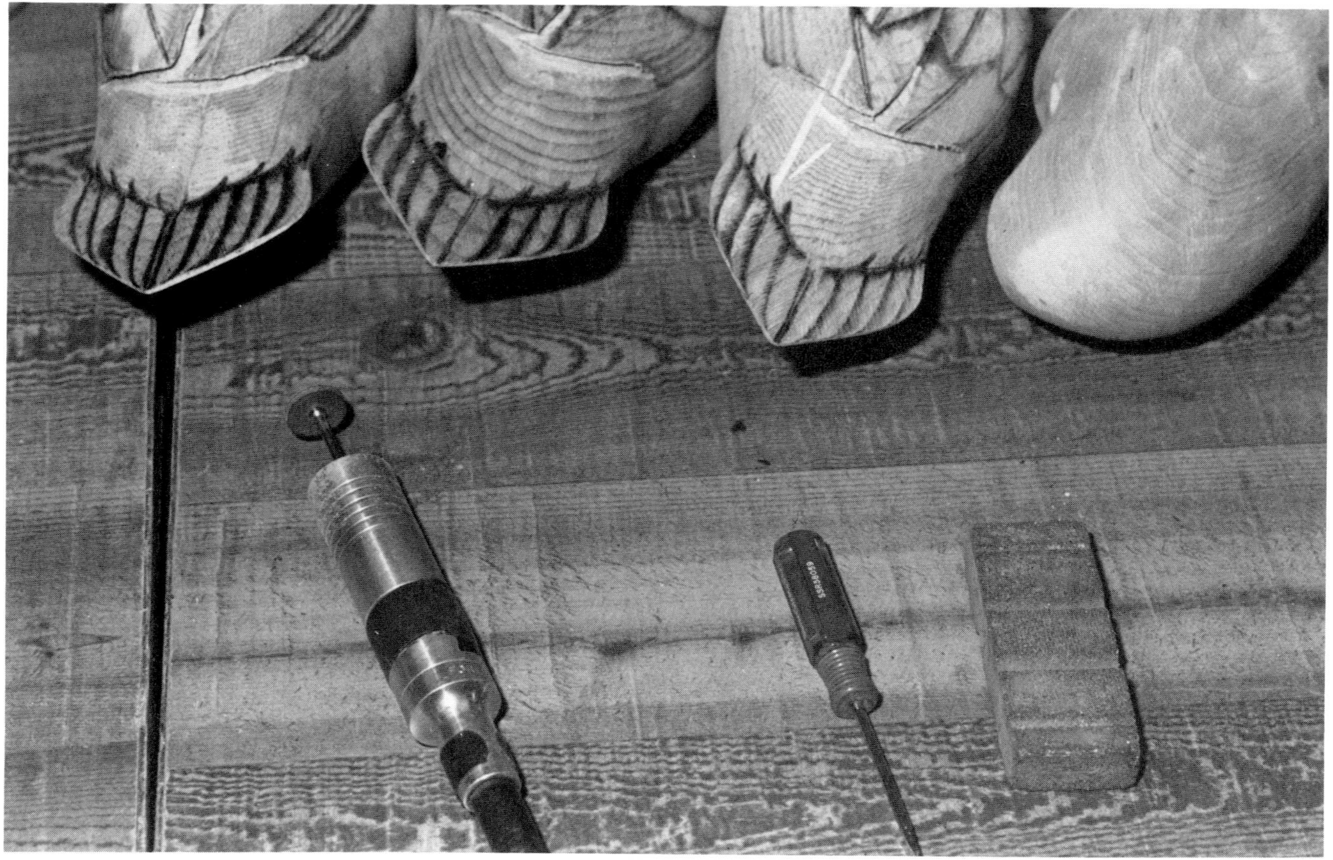

Example—discs, stone and birds for texturing

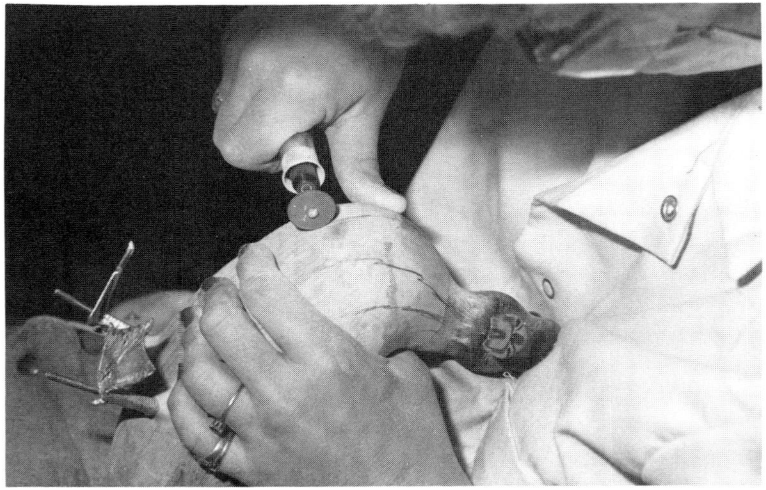
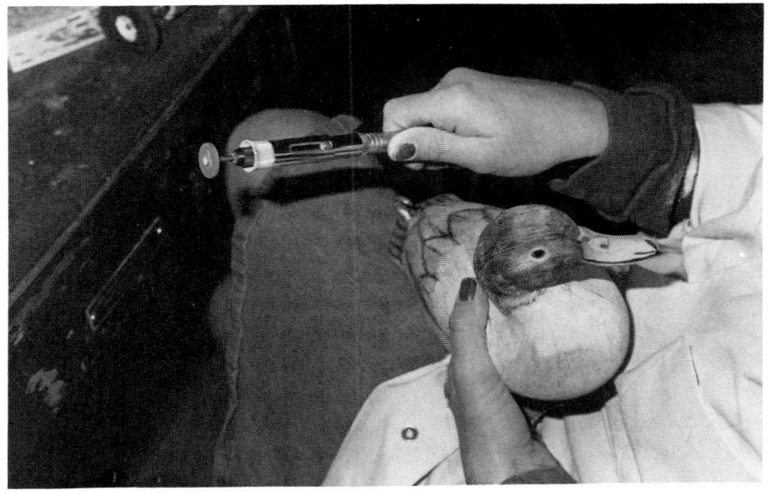

Example—texturing with discs using #8 handpiece

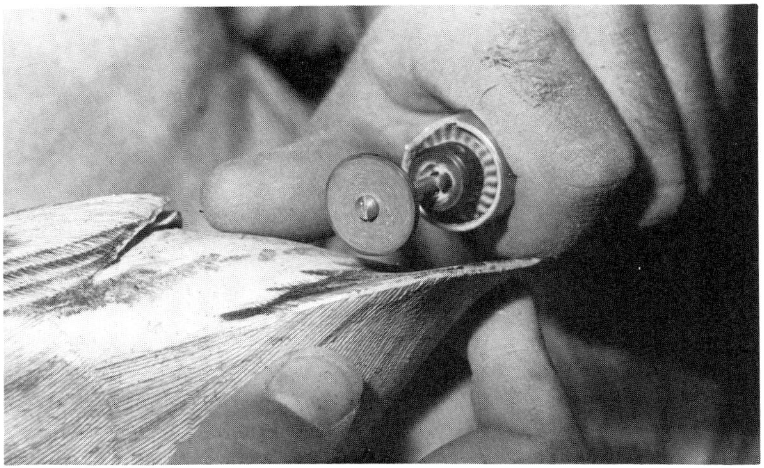

Example—texturing with discs using #30 handpiece

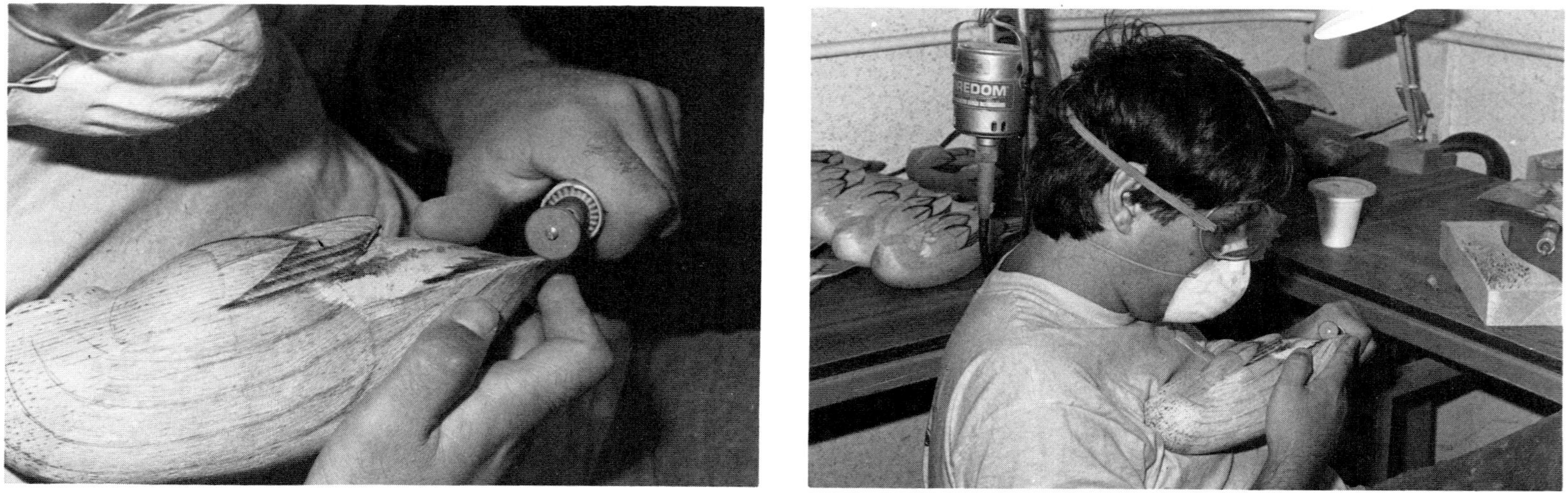

Example—texturing by left-handed person. Note: goggles and mask

Example—handpiece set up with small stone for texturing

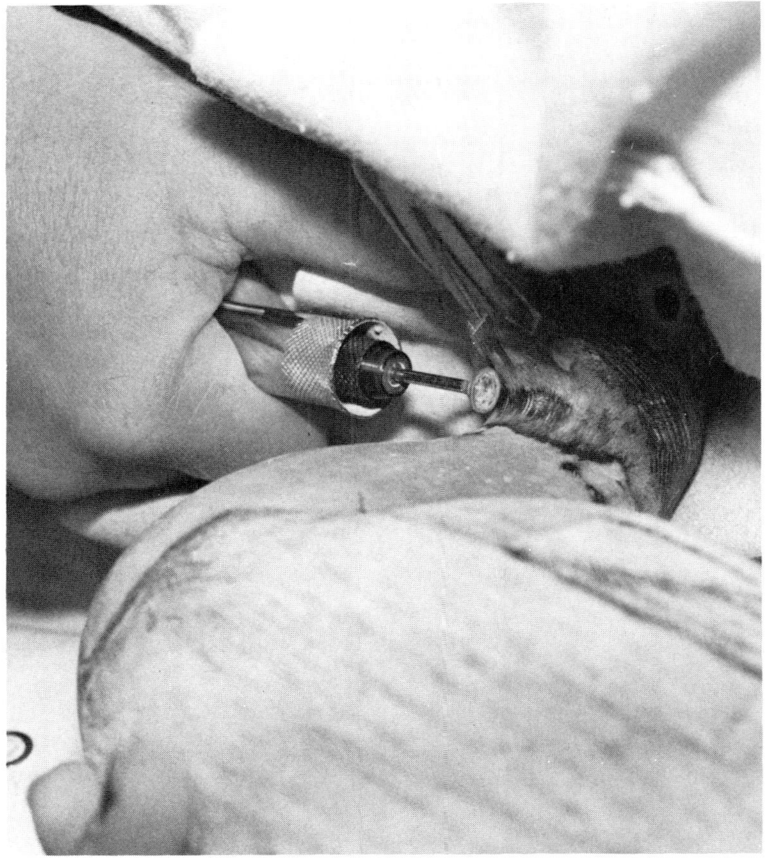

Example—texturing tight area with small stone

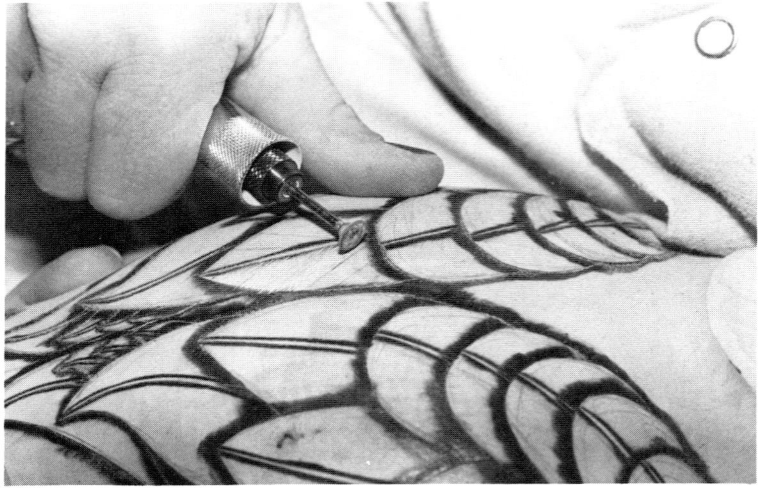

Example—texturing large feather grouping with small stone

Texturing wing area with stone—note: that primaries and secondaries have been burned—a combination of different texturing methods is sometimes desirable for special effects

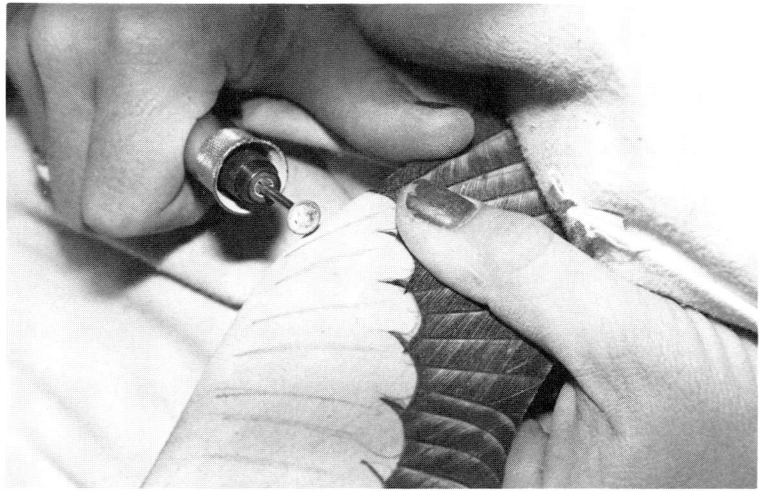

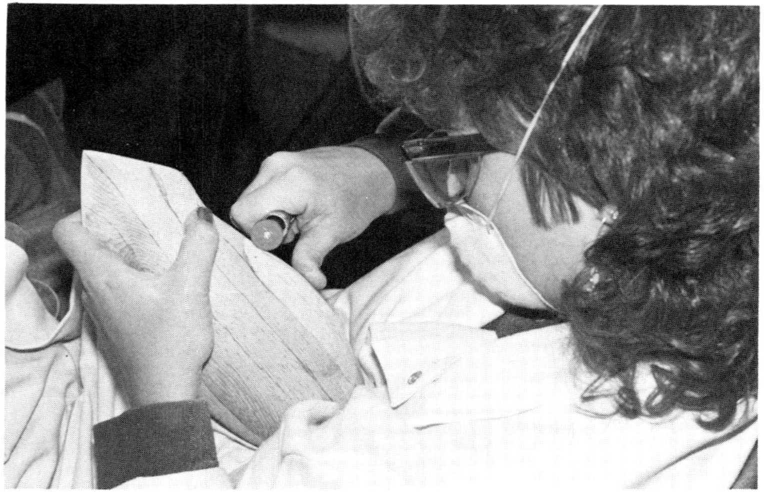

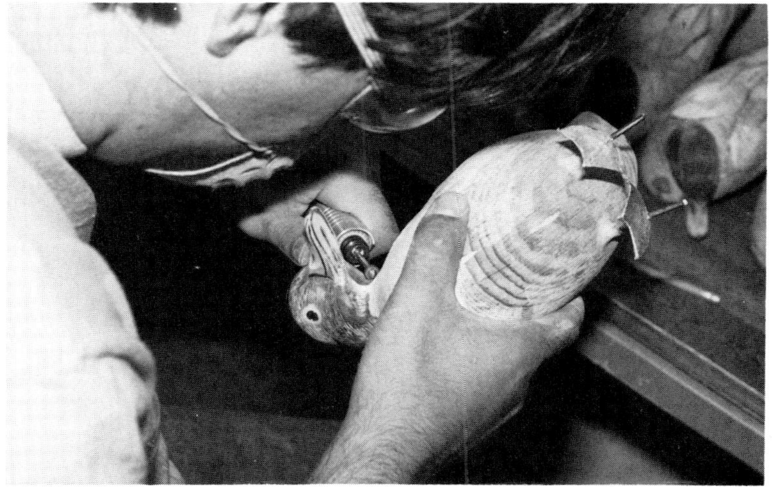

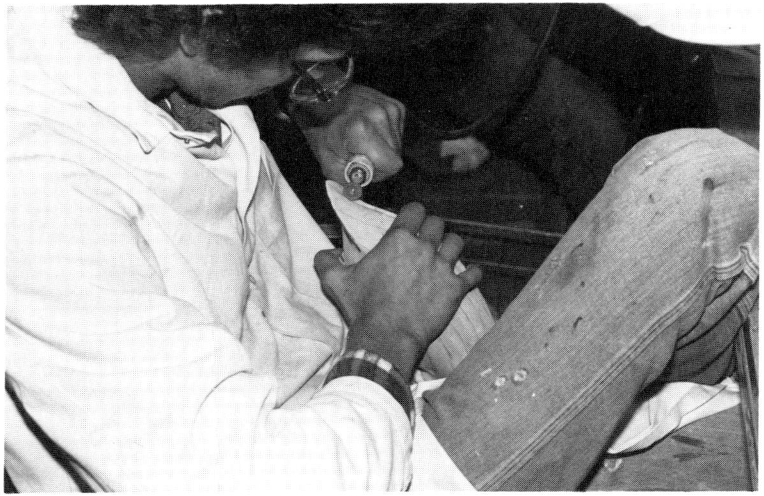

More examples of texturing and how to hold for different areas.
Be comfortable

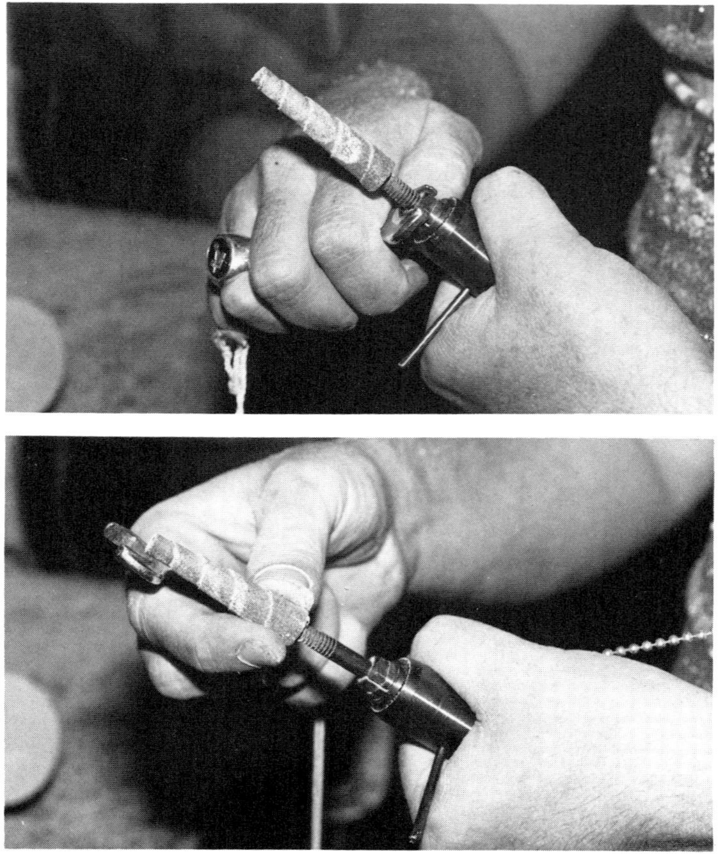

Example—cartridge sander for die grinder handpiece

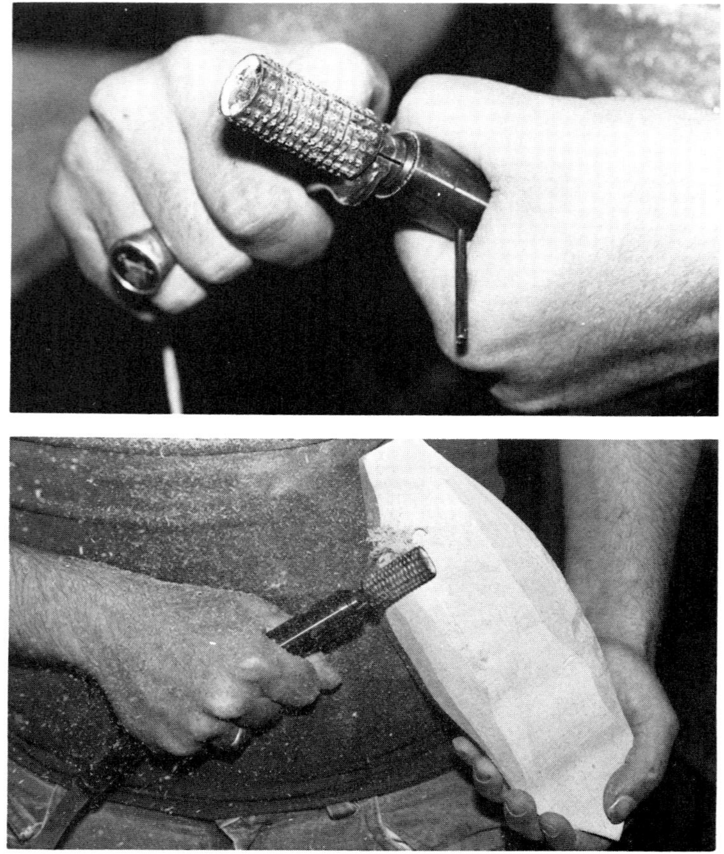

Example—3/4" Arco hollow rasps in die grinder handpieces.

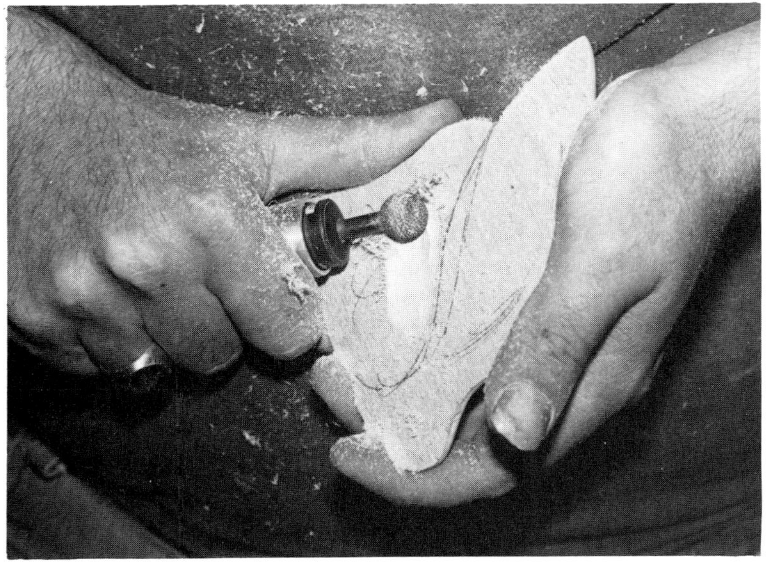 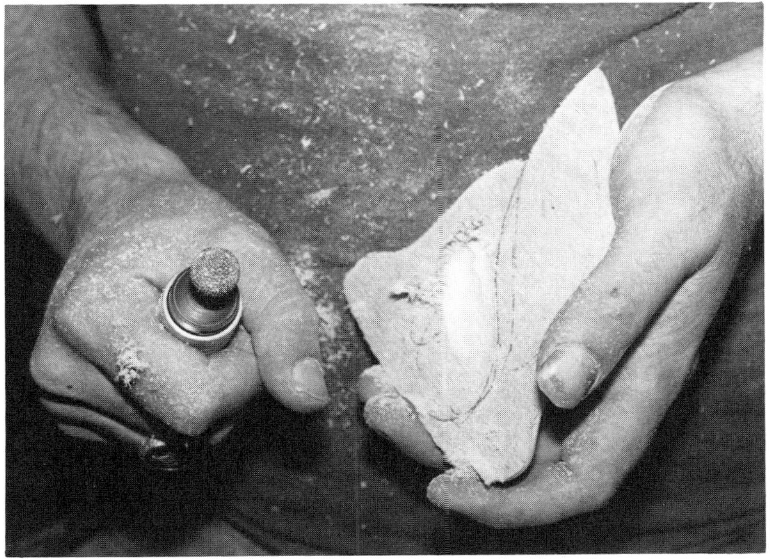

Example—using 1/2" Karbide Kutzall to hollow under wing using 44B handpiece.

Note: The foredom flexade shaft is a good shaft for your die grinder and will enable you to use your foredom handpiece on a limited basis, or you can buy high speed foredom handpieces if you do a great deal of work.

Example—set of collets for 44B handpiece

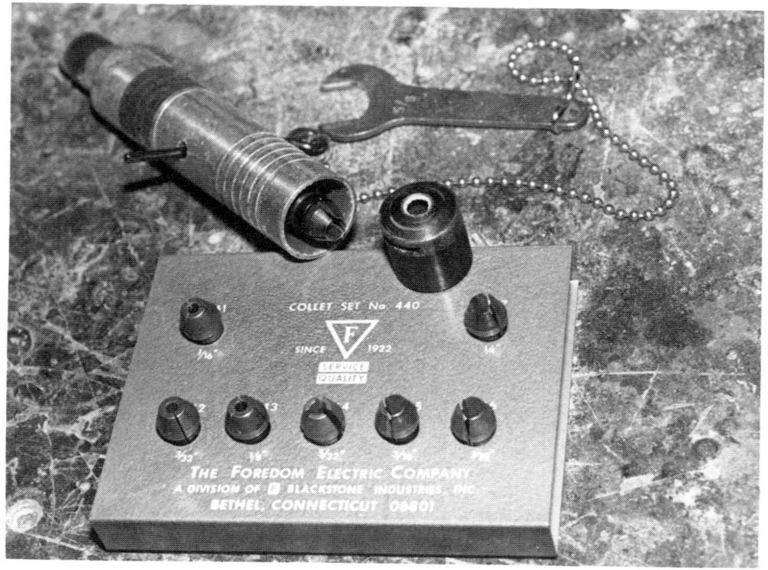

Example—set of collets for 44B handpiece plus handpiece

Example—44B handpiece with 3/4" Arco hollow rasp

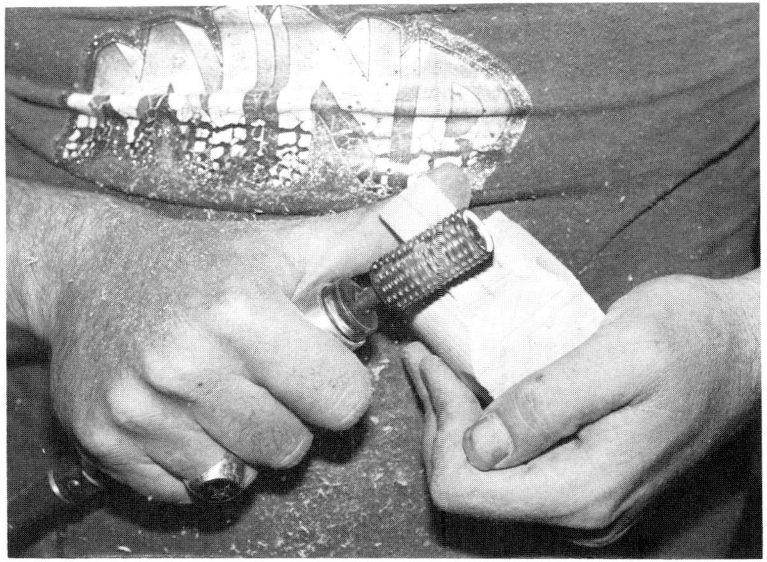

Example—carving bill with 3/4" Arco rasp

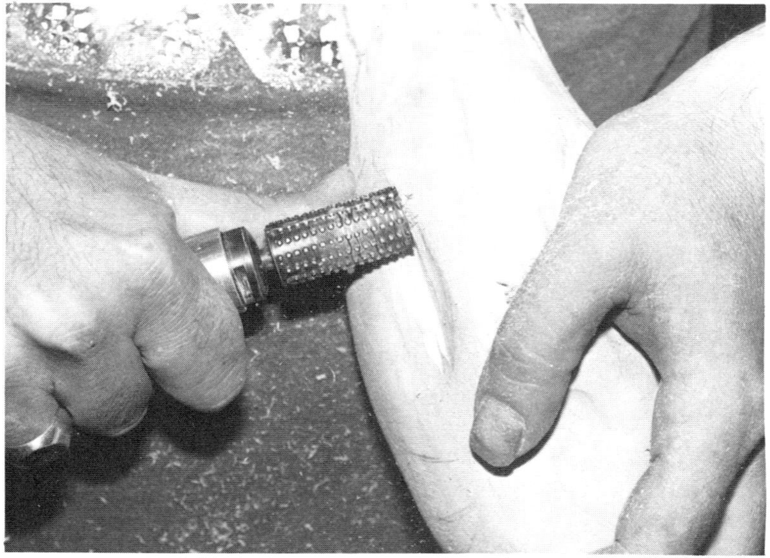

Example—carving side pocket with 3/4'' Arco rasp

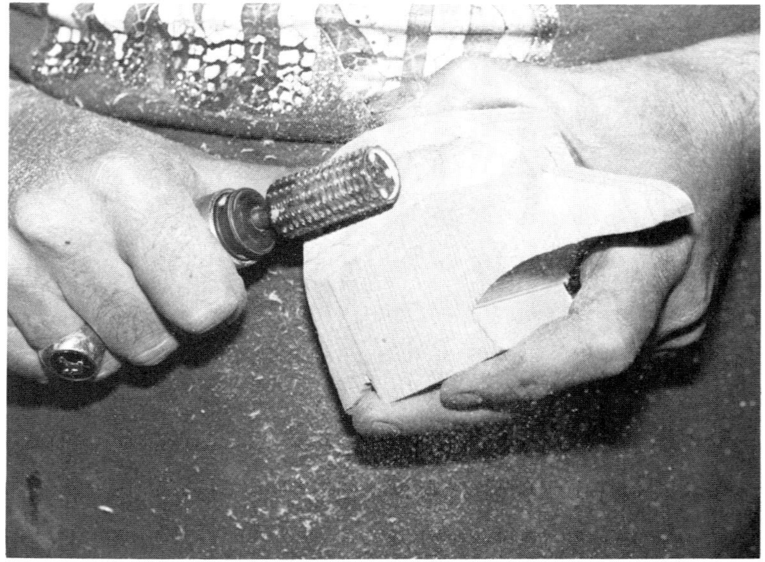

Example—carving eye channel with 3/4'' Arco rasp

Example—flap sanders in 44B handpiece

Example—assortment of bits and sander with 1/4" shank

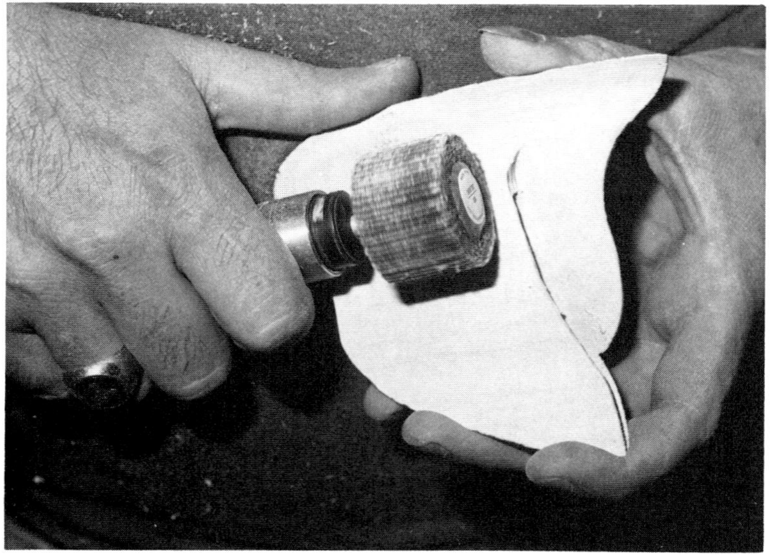

Example—flap sanders on underside of wing

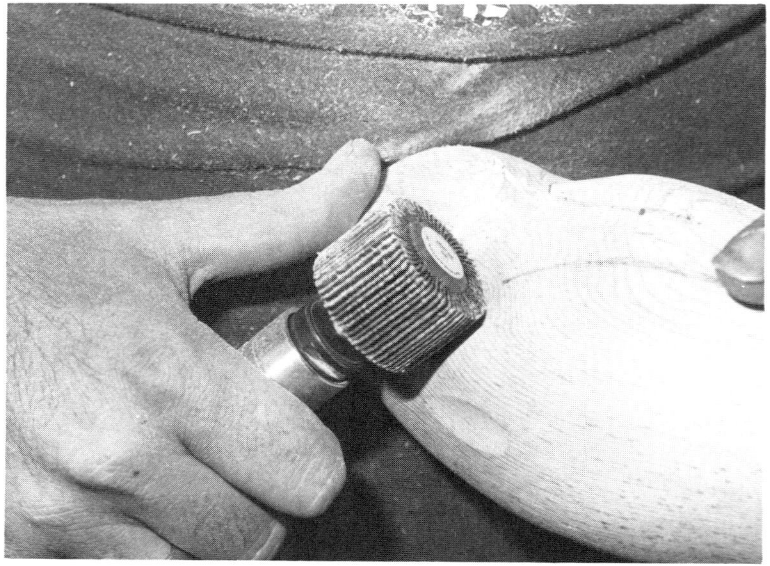

Example—flap sander sanding chest area

Example—fine sanding with special cartridge roll on chest and fill area

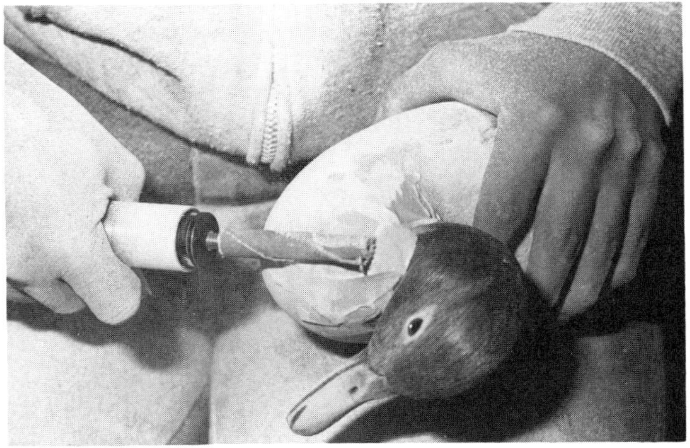

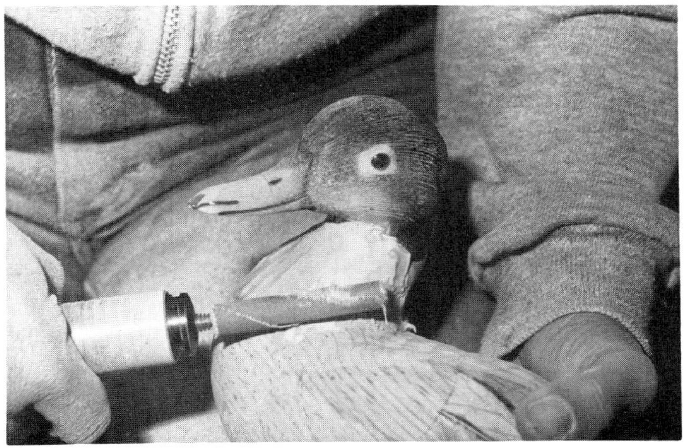

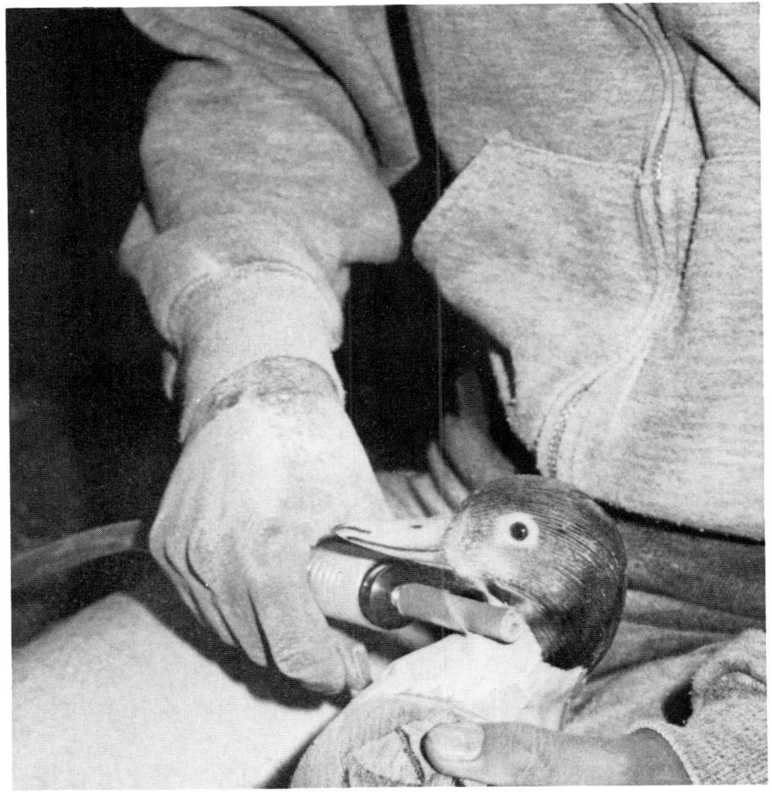

Example—fine sanding with special cartridge roll under chin and neck area

Example—setting cartridge roll mandrel in 44B handpiece

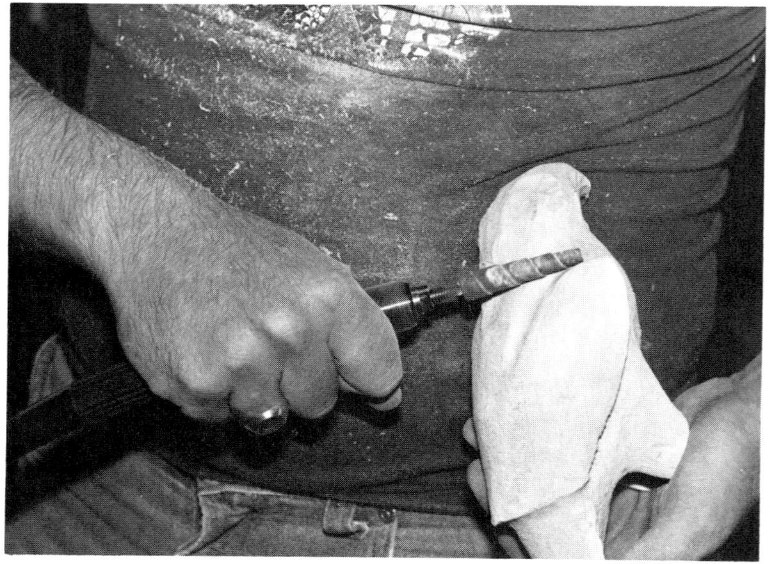

Example—sanding with tapered cartridge roll

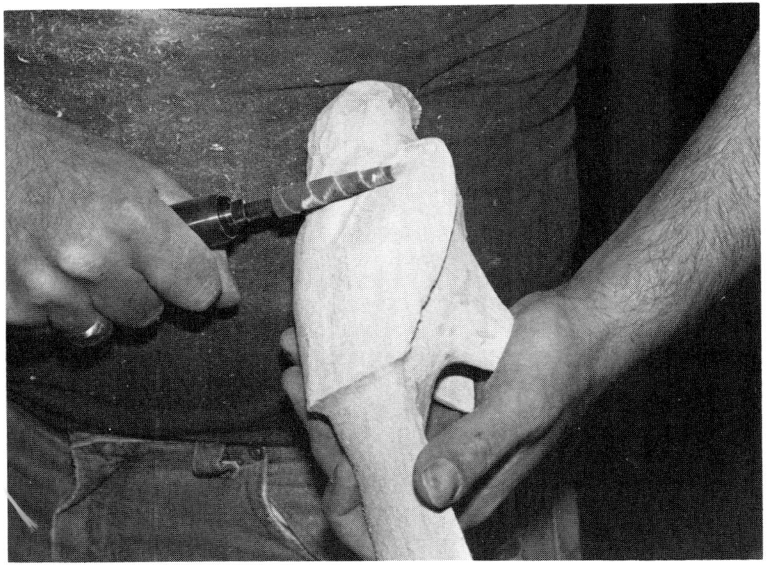

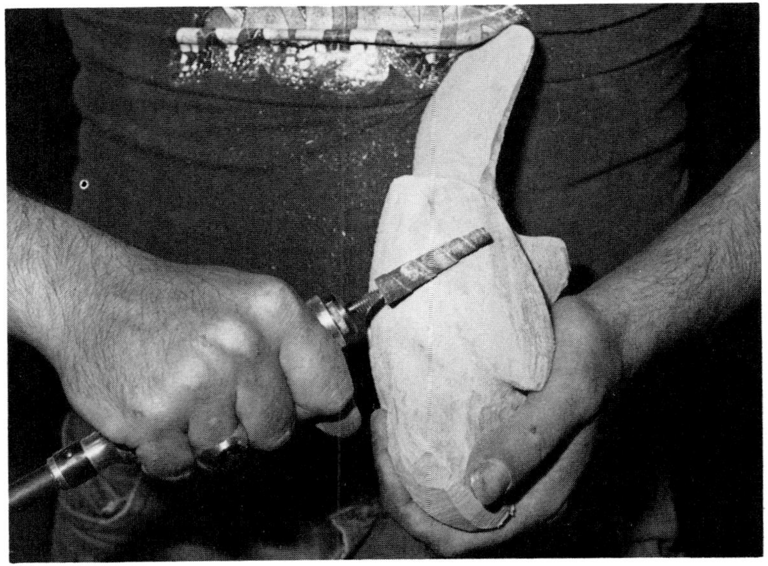

Further examples of sanding different areas with tapered cartridge roll

Example—foredom hanging on hanger with 44B handpiece and 3/4" Karbide taper bit for heavy grinding

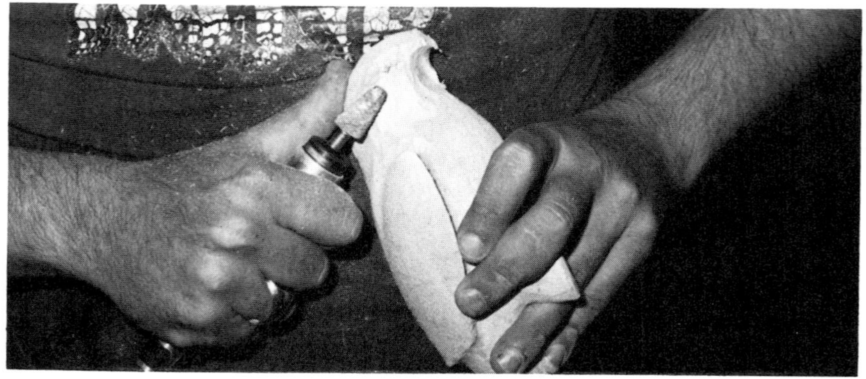

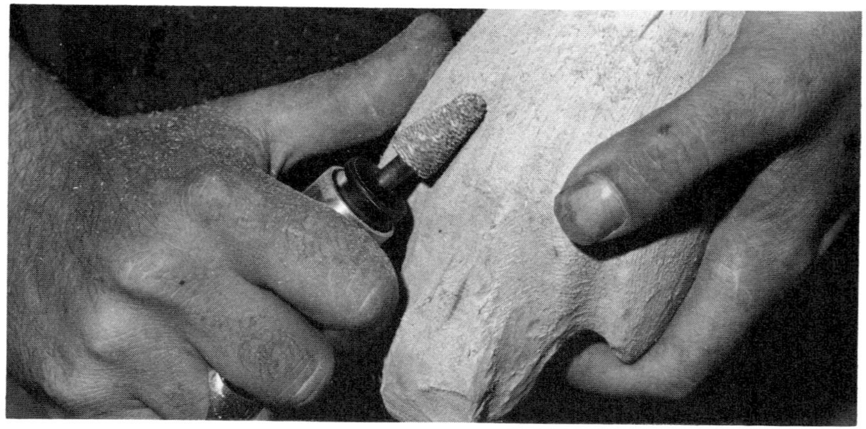

Example—using 3/4" tapered Karbide for shaping especially indented areas

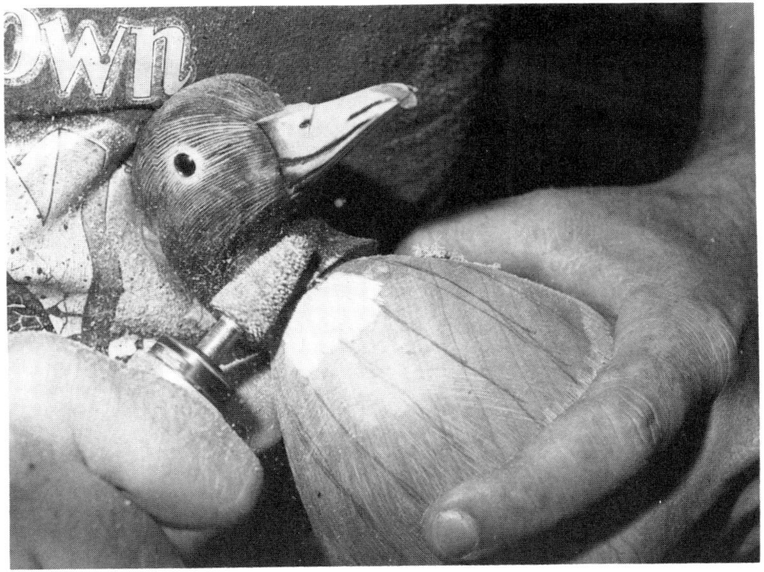

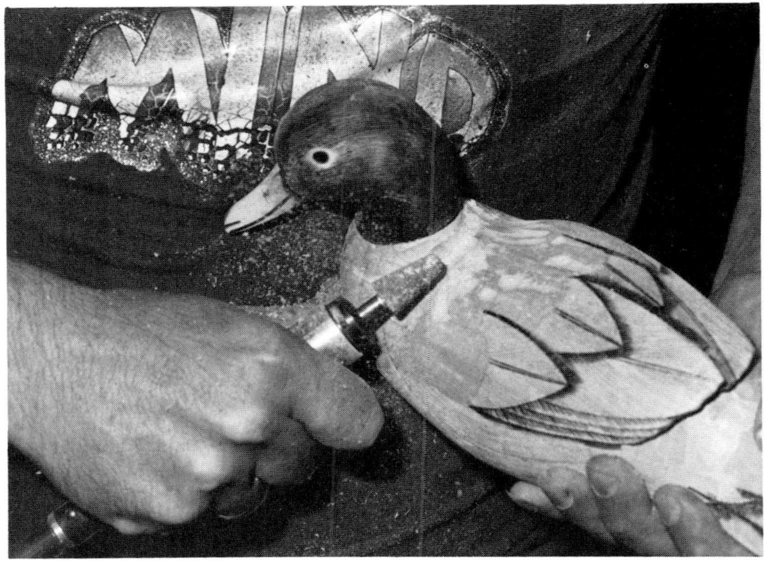

Example—shaping neck joint area with 3/4" tapered Karbide prior to filling

Example—further shaping of neck joint

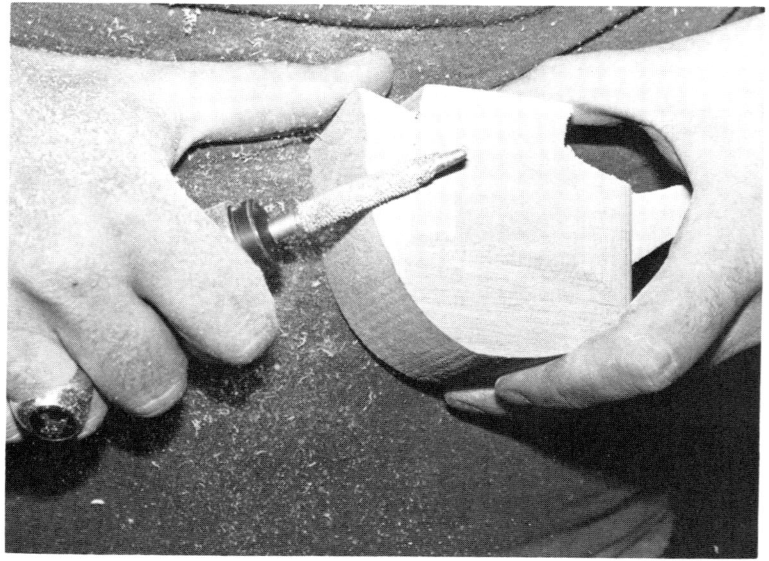

Example—carving with 1/2" long taper

Other wood carving books from Schiffer Publishing Ltd.

Championship Carving, Tricia Veasey and Tom Johnson. The winning carvings of the 1984 Ward Foundation World Championship carving competitions have been superbly photographed and compiled here. 400 stunning color pictures of professional and world-class carvings accompany an informative and authoritative series of interviews with this year's finest sculptors of wood.

Championship Carving allows you to examine blue ribbon carvings at your leisure to discern what qualifies them as the best.

Novice and expert carvers will find this comprehensive volume, which is certain to become a collector's item, to be an indispensible addition to their libraries.

Blue Ribbon Techniques: Burning and Texturing Methods, William Veasey. Effective burning techniques separate the artists from the amateurs. Burning techniques have often been neglected in carving literature, but burning, like carving and painting, is an art in itself. William Veasey, master carver and teacher, realised that a need for a comprehensive book on burning techniques existed, and characteristically decided to answer that need.

Blue Ribbon Burning Techniques will show you how to use your tools to achieve brilliant results. Crisp step-by-step photographs and instructions will enable the beginner to detail his carvings with a minimum of difficulty and magnificent results. It will give the expert blue ribbon ideas that will make the difference between a good carving and the best of show.

Get the technique — your blue ribbon is waiting for you.

Complete Waterfowl Studies, Bruce Burk. This is a major new work of great importance to all bird carvers, painters, taxidermists, naturalists, and other bird lovers. A comprehensive, in-depth, photographic study of North American waterfowl, this study is covered by three volumes. Selections from the author's large collection of waterfowl photographs help the artist accurately duplicate the incomparable beauty and grace of our ducks, geese, and swans. These photographs, over 96% published here for the first time, show structural detail and body form taken from many different angles. Our waterfowl are pictured here in almost every conceivable position on land, on water, and in the air. Artists can now, by referring to just one source, obtain a great selection of usable poses, all carefully selected by the author for their artistic value.

Volume I: *Dabbling and Whistling Ducks,* covers our most colorful group of waterfowl—ducks of the ponds, lakes, and rivers.

Volume II: *Diving Ducks* covers our ducks of the deeper waters, often salty, who have marvelously adapted themselves to feeding below the surface, sometimes at incredible depths.

Volume III: *Geese and Swans* covers our goose and swan species of North America, plus the nene goose of Hawaii, the barnacle goose of Europe, the beautiful little red-breasted goose and lesser white-fronted goose of Europe and Asia, and the mute swan which is native of Europe.

Bills and Feet: An Artisan's Handbook, William Veasey and Sina Kurman. This long-awaited artist's manual is the first definitive sourcebook of its kind. In it, William Veasey teaches decorative decoy artists to accurately paint the details of waterfowl and gamebird bills and feet, as well as those of birds of prey. *Bills and Feet* is an authoritative work which will allow the craftsman to achieve a more lifelike effect with his carvings. Illustrated in full color, it is a must for the serious decoy artist.

Waterfowl Illustrated, Tricia Veasey. There is now available a beautiful waterfowl source book for carvers, taxidermists, ornithologists, and waterfowl enthusiasts by the accomplished carver/photographer Tricia Veasey. Close-up photographs in color and black and white show detailed feather patterns, color, detail, and species conformation. Full species descriptions accompany these beautiful and important illustrations. A comprehensive state-by-state guide for where to observe the waterfowl in natural habitats includes national and local wildlife refuges, zoos and other preserves.

Decoy Carving Techniques for the Intermediate Carver, George Barber and Larry Reader. This illustrated sourcebook focuses on competition carving, and carving for the decoy market. It includes detailed, easy-to-follow descriptions of feathering methods, planning techniques, and for assembling a carved bird. Barber discusses the best tools and the outlets from which they can be obtained. The novice carver is given sufficient information on tools and techniques to raise his carving skills to the intermediate level; and to instill his carvings with a dynamic realism which will make them difficult to distinguish from their live counterparts.

The Carver's Handbook, Volume I: Wood Carving the Wonders of Nature, David Pergrin. With the help of this book, you will be able to transform a block of bass wood into a chickadee poised for flight, a chipmunk nibbling a nut, a ponderous box turtle, or a relief carving of the Holy Family.

Thorough instructions in pictures and text guide you through each phase of the carving process, from cutting out the rough shape on the bandsaw or handsaw to the final shaping to painting the finest details. Helpful tips will enable you to complete even your first project with ease and expertise.

The Carver's Handbook, Volume II: Carving the Wild Life of the Forest and Jungle, David E. Pergrin. This second volume in the Carver's Handbook series gives instructions for carvers to make and paint wooden figures of a tiger, an American goldfinch, and a wood mouse in the round and a great horned owl in relief. The instructions are given with step-by-step suggestions and illustrations. Each project is introduced with a list of all the tools and materials needed for that figure.

The Carvers' Handbook, Volume III: Woodcarving Wild Animals, David E. Pergrin. Wood carvers now have patterns and clear instructions for making life-like images of a Cardinal bird, trotting horse, standing deer and an Indian with headdress neckerchief slide. These projects are taught in this third volume of the successful Carvers' Handbook series through 78 step-by-step pictures and carefully written instructions. 27 clear color photographs show each stage of painting for these popular projects. Mr. Pergrin shares his teaching experience and award-winning carving skills to enable craftsmen of all levels of experience to make their own fine carvings.